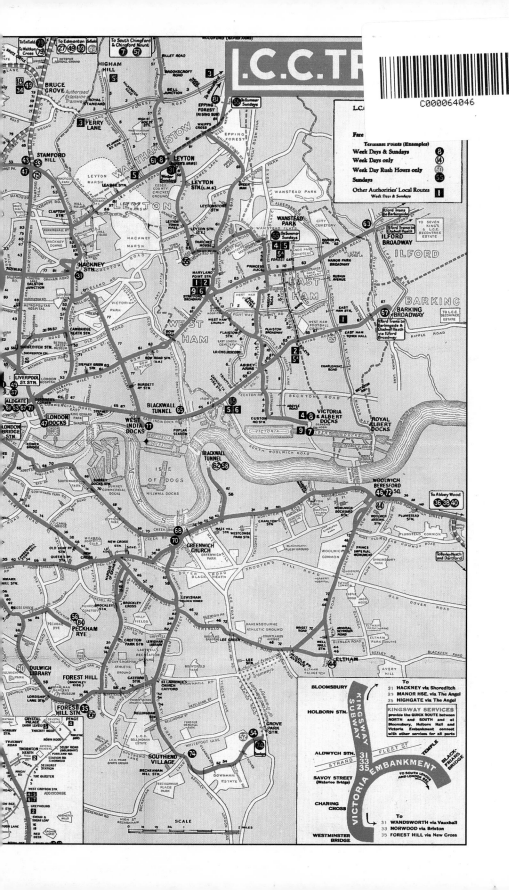

London Trams

A VIEW FROM THE PAST

PAUL COLLINS

PUBLISHING

Front cover: Shadows are cast on a sunny day in May 1949 as 'E/1' car No 1395 accelerates away from Gresham Road change pit in Brixton, having moved on to an overhead wire section of route 34 Blackfriars-Battersea Bridge. Shadows of the late war can be seen in the car's headlamp mask and the white bands on the bollards. The car was one of 29 withdrawn with the closure of route 34 on 30 September 1950.
W. E. Robertson via Leeds Transport Historical Society

Back cover top: The Metropolitan Electric Tramways' 'Feltham' cars entered service between 1 February and 29 October 1931. No 362 was based at Finchley and worked the 21 route Holborn-North Finchley. She is seen in Holbotn in July 1932.
National Tramway Museum

Back cover bottom: On summer Sundays LT's route 6 City-Tooting (Amen Corner) was extended to Mitcham (Fair Green), where, on Sunday 4 October 1936 No 1664 is seen. In 1936 the route extension operated between 14 June and 18 October. Thirteen months later the car was fitted with vestibule screens and she remained in service until February 1952.
H. F. Wheeler/R. S. Carpenter

Title page: This ex-MET Type H (LPTB No 2237) is working route 19 to Barnet on 26 December 1935, at the Tottenham Court Road/Hampstead Road junction, on a conduit section of the route, which closed for conversion to trolleybus operation on 6 March 1938. Deployed elsewhere, No 2237 remained in service until November 1938.
H. F. Wheeler/R. S. Carpenter

First published 2001

ISBN 0 7110 2741 2

Published by Ian Allan Publishing

an imprint of Ian Allan Publishing Ltd, Shepperton, Surrey TW17 8AS.
Printed by Ian Allan Printing Ltd, Hersham, Surrey KT12 4RG.

Code: 0101/B

Below: A Class F subway car, one of 16 such cars (Nos 552-567) built in 1905 for the opening of the Kingsway Subway. One in the 55x series is seen posed outside The Artificial Teeth Institute, F. J. Collins' (no relation) Electric Light Studio, and a Marks & Spencer Original Penny Bazaar.
London Transport Museum

Below right: An unidentified 'HR/2' of *circa* 1931 displays the new Pullman livery of red and cream, plus the equal-wheel bogies which gave the cars their great traction for working hilly routes. On the front dash side the car declares itself to be 'ONE OF 150 NEW AND BETTER TRAMS FOR SOUTH LONDON'. *London Transport Museum*

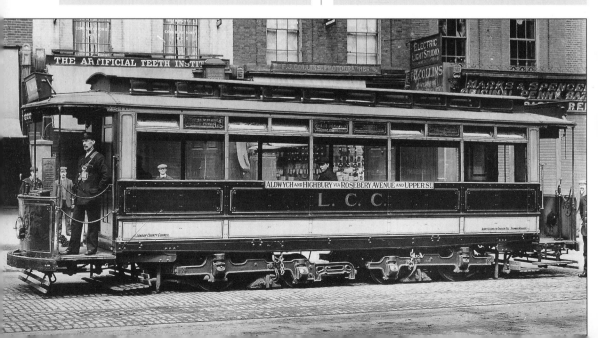

Contents

Acknowledgements

I am very grateful to the following individuals and organisations, without whose help this book would not have been possible: John Bradshaw, Roger Carpenter, June Collins, Ray Cresswell and Brierley Office Products, East Ham Library, Mellanie Hartland, the library of the Ironbridge Gorge Museum Trust, Stella Jamieson, the staff at the London Transport Museum, Simon Murphy, Steven Parascandolo, Bronwen Reid, Science Museum, Peter Skidmore, and the staff at the Library of the University of Birmingham.

I also wish to give special thanks to Paul Cripps, Nick Grant and Peter Waller at Ian Allan Publishing Ltd for their patience and forbearance, and to Winston Bond, Rosie Thacker, and Glyn Wilton of the National Tramway Museum, for all of their help and support with this project.

Paul Collins MSc, MSocSci, PhD
Wollaston, Stourbridge, West Midlands
December 2000

By the late 1930s there were very few tram routes left operating north of the Thames, most having been replaced by trolleybuses. The three longest were those working through the Kingsway Subway — routes 31, 33 and 35. 'E/3' class cars working routes 31 and 33 are seen here at High Street, Islington, looking towards Islington Green, towards which a distant trolleybus is headed. *IAL*

Introduction

When I was about 12, I saw a short piece of film on television showing London trams on the Embankment. Inconsequential enough, but that was sufficient to spark my interest in trams.

The year 2000 is a good vantage-point from which to look back at London's trams. It is almost half a century since the last tram ran in London, and is the same year that the first of its next generation of trams entered service in Croydon.

Today we view London trams with the same curious mix of affection and nostalgia which we reserve for much of our 'heritage'. But how were they seen and regarded in the past? What did people think of them when they were new, or showing their age, or being withdrawn?

This book is an attempt to view London trams from the past, as they were seen at the various stages in their history and development. The accounts drawn upon have been found, in the main, in the trade and engineering press of the last 140 years or so, and include *The Journal of the Institute of Electrical Engineers, The Engineer, Engineering, Proceedings of the Institute of Civil Engineers, The Light Railway & Tramway Journal, Modern Transport, Passenger Transport, The Electric Railway & Tramway Journal* and *The Electric Railway, Bus & Tram Journal.*

This is not intended to be a history — definitive or otherwise — of London trams. Others, with much more time and space at their disposal, have gone that way before. Instead, this book is intended to travel through time with London trams, and, wherever possible, to tell things how they were. Above all, I hope that something of the people who devoted their lives to building, operating and riding London trams comes over. Public transport isn't about vehicles, it's about people. Have a pleasant journey!

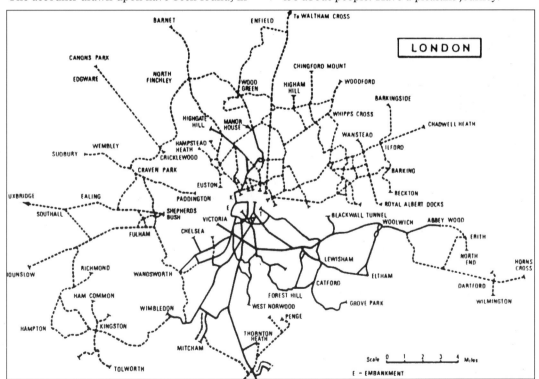

Above: This handsome lithograph adorned the front of Train's pamphlet. Sometimes mistaken for a view of the Bayswater Road line in operation, it was in fact prepared in Liverpool in 1860. Train's line never quite reached Marble Arch, it was not a double track (see foreground, right), and double-deck cars were not used. In his text Train referred to this illustration thus: 'The Lithograph of the Railway in operation may tend to remove the impression of the Irish Times, of a long line of carriages and a shrieking locomotive whirling through a crowded city; and may also answer the question, "Do you intend a stationary engine at Leece-street, Liverpool, or High Holborn, London; or do you propose to tunnel the hills?" Therefore the picture may explain better than the pamphlet; observations being quicker than reflection; the eyes satisfied, the ears are content.' *Author's collection*

Below: The front of the menu card for the Yankee Breakfast held to commemorate the opening of Train's Victoria Street line at 10.00am on 15 April 1861. Note how the familiar lithograph has been subtly altered for the occasion. The seven-course breakfast included 'Pig's Feet Saint Menehould', 'Dropped Eggs', 'Reindeer Tongue' and 'Baba Cakes', ideal fare for a tram ride.
National Tramway Museum

1. 'A boon to the people...' — Trams come to London by Train

At least twice, late in 1857 and early in 1858, the wheels of carriages carrying the MP Sir Benjamin Hall, Bt, were wrenched off as they crossed colliery tramway lines in his former Monmouth constituency. Sir Benjamin was shaken by these incidents, and stirred, into a passionate hatred of 'tramways' that came to haunt early attempts to build them in London.

Londoners had shown little spontaneous interest in tramways, and the re-laying of part of Commercial Road with stepped-block paving in 1829, literally to 'channel' the movement of carts and wagons, is the only tram-like development that can be identified before the late 1850s.

Elsewhere, the horse-drawn omnibus and street railway had been developed, respectively in Paris and New York, in the years either side of 1830. Twenty years later, a Frenchman, Alphonse Loubat, who had built street railways in New York, conceived the idea of a hybrid 'tram-bus'. On his return to France in 1852, Loubat petitioned the Parisian authorities for permission to build a line to Boulogne. This opened in 1853, using vehicles with flat-tyred wheels, for running in the streets, which converted to ones with flanges, for running along track outside the city.

Loubat's innovations inspired two attempts to introduce tram-buses to London. The first came from Paris, where, in 1855, the city's various omnibus interests were combined into a monopoly. Some involved in this saw London as another place where unifying omnibus interests would bring benefits. Later in 1855 they established the Compagnie Générale des Omnibus de Londres, which took over the existing omnibus firms, commencing operation in January 1856. The following year this 'London General Omnibus Co' set up the London Omnibus Tramway Co, incorporated on 13 October 1857, to build and operate horse tramways within a 20-mile radius of the General Post Office. A bill was lodged with Parliament, but this was defeated on its second reading, on 15 March 1858, largely through the vehement opposition of one Sir Benjamin Hall, now MP for Marylebone and Chief Commissioner of Works for London.

The second attempt was made by William Curtis, who, on a visit to Paris in 1855, became impressed with Loubat's line, and on his return to England set about improving the method of retracting the wheel flanges, which he patented in 1856. In March 1859, Curtis operated a car along a dock railway line in Liverpool, and by October 1860 he had tried, unsuccessfully, to lay a line along Liverpool Road, Islington.

In between these two attempts, London also received attention from a flamboyant American entrepreneur. George Francis Train was born in Boston on 24 March 1829. By his late 20s he had made a fortune from clipper ships. Train first encountered street railways in Philadelphia in the late 1850s. He recognised their potential and saw Europe as a market for them. Early in 1860, Train arrived in Liverpool and, that February, he petitioned the authorities to permit a demonstration line to be laid, but they regarded Curtis's line as a sufficient experiment, and so in March 1860 Train made similar approaches to the authorities in Birkenhead. These were received favourably, and on 7 May 1860 Train registered the Birkenhead Street Railway Co Ltd. Three months later, on 30 August 1860, he opened a 1¼-mile horse tramway line running from Woodside Ferry to Birkenhead Park.

Birkenhead was an able demonstration, but Train's ambitions lay elsewhere, as he wrote in 1860:

'When I made up my mind last year to succeed in demonstrating the practicability of these railways in English cities, London was the

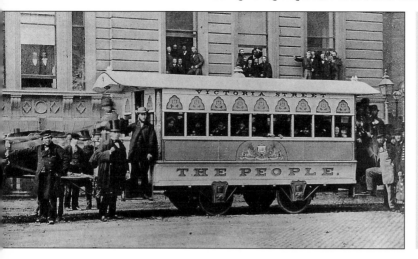

Only one of Train's three London lines seems to have been photographed, that along Victoria Street. This was most probably taken on the opening day — 15 April 1861 — possibly after the Yankee Breakfast. 'The People' seated 24, with a further 12 standees on each platform. Behind is an example of the fine six-storey Italianate buildings which lined Victoria Street when it was built in the late 1850s. Sadly, many of these were demolished when the street was redeveloped in the 1970s.
National Tramway Museum

starting point; but a member of Parliament assured me that most of the great undertakings of the day were initiated in the provinces, instancing "steamboats, railways, gas, water-works, telegraphs — even Rowland Hill was a provincial institution".'

To further his case, Train published a pamphlet, *Observations on Street Railways*, which was addressed to the Rt Hon Milner Gibson, MP, President of the Board of Trade. The following excerpts reveal much of Train's personality and approach. This is from the Preface:

'Street Railways in England will soon become a great fact — Birkenhead opens the ball. Liverpool follows. Then Manchester, Birmingham, Glasgow, and Dublin enter the ring; and London cannot well hold back after building the Metropolitan Subterranean Railway. A Street Railway can be constructed directly over it in as many months as that will require years. The former costs three thousand per mile, the latter three hundred thousand! In the one you travel in the dark, in the other in broad daylight. The Street Railway accommodates both sexes, while the Metropolitan shuts out one half the population — the ladies! (Who crosses in the Thames tunnel?) The former stops before everyman's door, the latter has stations only at intervals. One starts every five minutes, the other every half minute if required. The Metropolitan blocks up the thoroughfare for months, the Street

Railway for hours only. Surely then if London opens wide her gate to permit the Metropolitan to undermine the city, tunnel through sewers, water-pipes, gas-pipes, and cess-pools, at great cost and great inconvenience, she certainly will not shut it in my face when I respectfully ask permission for a fair trial of my Street Railway...?'

Train's own 'observations' formed the bulk of his pamphlet:

'Here is a picture. A wet day — every corner of the side-walk crowded with impatient pedestrians, each one anxiously peering up or down the street in search of the particular omnibus among the fifteen or twenty approaching, to carry him home, which, with as many more coming in the opposite direction, so effectually choke up the street, that the drays and carts unable to cross at the intersections, render the highway impassable to private vehicles, and are therefore driven to other streets, avoiding danger and delay; the omnibuses crowded to excess, cannot accommodate the vexed crowd on the side-walk, and the sudden halt with imminent risk of collision, with the drivers' "plenty of room, sir," with twenty inside — by no means softens the temper either of those in waiting, to those, who seated — not comfortably — look upon each moment of unnecessary delay, as an infringement of their rights.

'Here is another. Not an *omnibus* is seen in the whole length of the street — carriages, drays and carts move with comparative ease, little strips of iron are laid along the streets, upon and across which, vehicles pass without inconvenience, and, which, the drivers (particularly of private carriages) evidently seek; there is no crowd, for the little cars glide along rapidly and frequently, accommodating everybody; at a slight signal the bell rings, the horses stop, the passenger is comfortably seated, no rain drops in from the roof, the conductor is always ready to take the fare when offered, and the echo, "great improvement this," is constantly repeated.'

Train cited the following figures to support his case:

'One hundred and thirty-four omnibuses daily run to and from Paddington, Bayswater, and the city, via Holborn, Newgate-street, and Cheapside, making 1,312 journeys daily through those thoroughfares; and there are also thirty-four other omnibuses running to and from Bayswater, via Fleet-street, Ludgate-hill, and Cheapside, making 280 journeys daily; thus, practically to serve this district, 1,592 omnibuses, carrying about 25,000 passengers, daily pass through the most crowded streets in the city. In addition to the above, there is a continuous and increasing stream of cabs. The number of cabs in the Metropolis increased from 3,297, in 1852, to 4,505, in 1857.'

He also listed the following advantages of adapting omnibuses to tramways:

- one vehicle with two horses will carry 60 passengers, instead of 21, and the fares may be reduced 33%;
- the bulk of the traffic otherwise passing through narrow and crowded thoroughfares ... will be conveyed by the New and City-roads, in the same or less time than by the present route;
- ratepayers will be relieved of a portion of the tax for repairing the roads, as they will be saved the wear and tear of the omnibuses and horses which now pass over them;
- the wheels will be entirely removed from the road to the tramway, and the number of horses employed to carry the same number of

passengers as at present travel will be reduced one-third, and;
- the passage of the tramway omnibus on the smooth surface of the rail will be comparatively noiseless.

Train couldn't resist several jibes at Sir Benjamin Hall, based, largely, upon the London Omnibus Tramway Co's experience of him:

'The Cardinals endeavoured ... to make the sun revolve around the earth by imprisoning Galileo — learned professors saw no safety in Davy's lamp — distinguished physicians had no faith in Harvey's circulation ... . From Sir Benjamin's comments, he would have been among those clever men who ridiculed Watt's engine, sneered at Fulton's steamboat, and laughed at Stevenson's [sic] locomotive; but as these progressive minds triumphed over those who considered free trade in improvement criminal, so the practical working of Street Railways must succeed in making advocates of the theorists who do not understand them.'

Many at the time found Train to be 'brash', to have a 'glib tongue', and to 'yarn well'. All of these qualities come over in his writing. Was Train successful in introducing street railwats to London? Partly. By January 1861 he had decided to lay down a line along the Bayswater Road, and that month he registered the Marble Arch Street Rail Co Ltd. Agreement, rather than Parliamentary approval, was secured for the line that ran along Bayswater Road, from Porchester Terrace to Edgware Road — a distance of just under a mile — and opened on 23 March 1861, with a celebratory 'Turtle Lunch'. The cars were single-deck and seated 24, with a further 24 standees, 12 on each end platform.

On 15 April 1861 Train opened a second line along Victoria Street, a newly-formed road that connected Whitehall with Vauxhall Bridge Road through an area of former slum housing. The day was attended by some ceremony, and a 'Yankee Breakfast' was held at the Westminster Palace Hotel at 10.00am. The company that operated the line — The Westminster Street Rail Co Ltd — was not, however, registered until 22 April 1861.

Four months later, on 15 August 1861,

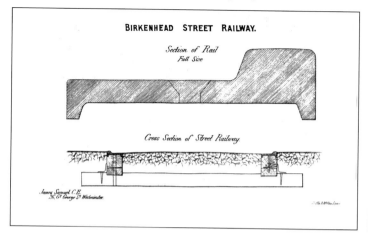

BIRKENHEAD STREET RAILWAY.

Section of Rail
Full Size

Cross Section of Street Railway

Train's tramways used a form of step rail, which was illustrated in his pamphlet. The rail is a metal strap, spiked to a wooden bearer and sleeper. Despite his declaration that these would 'be perfectly flush with the general surface of the roadway, and will not in any way interfere with the passage along and across it of any ordinary road waggon, or carriage', in practice they stood several inches proud of the road surface and were a considerable nuisance to other road users. *Author's collection*

Train's third and final London demonstration line opened, from Westminster Bridge to Kennington Gate, this being operated by the Surrey Side Street Rail Co Ltd (registered 29 May 1861). In five months Train had three demonstration lines working in London. They were a hit with the public but less popular with the competition and other road users. Train's tramways used 'step rails', which bore a flange that stood proud of the roadway, and were single lines laid on one side of the road, so that when working in one direction his vehicles were moving against the prevailing flow of traffic. Complaints mounted, notably from the not

disinterested London General Omnibus Co, and in September 1861 the Bayswater line closed. Similar disputes forced the closure of the Victoria Street line on 6 March 1862 and the Westminster Bridge one on 21 June 1862, the latter whilst workers were tearing up the lines.

History has tended to view George Francis Train's three short London lines as something of a failure. Nonetheless, they operated for around 800 days, and, extrapolating from available figures, in that time they carried in excess of 2 million people, ran over 180,000 miles, and took almost £20,000 in fares — not a bad failure!

Rides on Train's lines could be booked in advance by the purchase of brass tokens. Examples of two of these survive, for the Marble Arch and Surrey Side lines. *National Tramway Museum*

2. Putting their shoulders to it — London's horse trams

Tickets issued for London's Last Tram Week in July 1952 proudly claimed 91 years of service for the capital's trams, between the then present and Train's lines of 1861. It all made for snappy copy on the back of the tickets, but it overlooked the seven years, 10 months and two weeks that London was without any trams at all.

Moves to reintroduce tramways to London began late in 1865 when the Metropolitan Tramways Co was formed. It tried to obtain Parliamentary powers in 1866 and 1867, but was ruled out of even lodging a bill. More success followed in 1868 (coincidentally the year after Sir Benjamin Hall's death), when its bill gained its second reading, but was defeated. By 1869, there were five tramways open in the rest of the country, and Parliament anticipated powers being sought for more and more schemes by proposing and passing a general Tramways Act in 1870.

It was against this background that in 1869 three new companies proposed tramways in London: north of the Thames there was the North Metropolitan Tramways Co, and to the south were the Metropolitan Street Tramways

Co and Pimlico, Peckham & Greenwich Street Tramways Co. Each obtained its act, and the first to open was the Metropolitan Street Tramways Co, which, on 2 May 1870, had the singular honour of opening London's first grooved-rail street tramway, on its Brixton–Kennington route. One week later the North Metropolitan Tramways Co opened its Whitechapel–Bow route, and on 13 December 1870 the Pimlico, Peckham & Greenwich Street Tramways Co opened its Blackheath Hill–New Cross line.

From this point on there was a veritable explosion in the number of tramway companies and lines. Some were very short in both length and existence, others merged to form larger companies based upon a common territory, whilst a few just grew and grew. The North Metropolitan alone opened a further 46 lines between 1 March 1871 and 1 August 1901. It was the largest single company before the formation of the London County Council (LCC) in 1889 and its subsequent acquisition of tramway undertakings. The North Metropolitan's figures for 1898 show that it

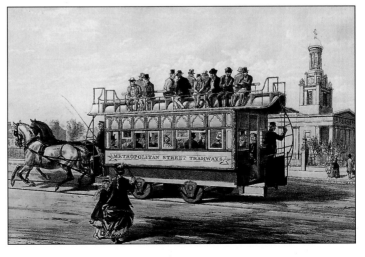

An illustration of the Metropolitan Street Tramway's first line between Brixton and Kennington, which opened on 2 May 1870, being London's first grooved-rail street tramway. The car has somewhat generous knifeboard seating on the top deck, which overhangs the platforms at both ends. Behind is Kennington Church.
National Tramway Museum

alone had almost 52 miles of lines, 673 tramcars, and 7,167 horses with which to work them.

Overall, by the dawn of the 20th century, London had 142 miles of tramways, all but a few of which were worked by horses. These laid the basis for the electrification schemes that were to follow shortly. The circumstances and dealings which led to these tramways being built, operated, traded and converted to electric traction are well documented elsewhere. Much rarer are contemporary accounts of the working of London's horse trams. One such survives from 1902, the eve of electrification for many lines. This is adapted from a book on *Living London*, published that year:

'During the hours which elapse between the arrival of the first tram at Aldgate, crowded with working men, and the departure suburbwards of the last 'bus, loaded with cheerful folk fresh from an after-theatre supper, cabs, 'buses, and trams carry between them all classes of His Majesty's subjects, from the peer and the millionaire to the coster and the workhouse woman.

'Let us begin by seeing the trams at work. It is eight a.m., and at the entrance to a big North London tramyard stand some eight or nine smartly-uniformed conductors and leather-aproned drivers discussing the latest news. Close by, in the yard inspector's office, are three conductors receiving their boxes of tickets, and signing for them in a big many-columned book. A car comes slowly from the back of the yard, and the men at the gate stand aside to let it pass. A conductor jumps on it, dons his bell-punch, and prepares for work. In less than a minute the car is at the starting-point, where clerks, shop assistants, office boys, and tea-shop girls have been anxiously awaiting its arrival. Several youths and one girl jump on the car before it stops; the others wait until it is at a standstill. Then ten of them attempt to step on the platform at the same time, and not a little pushing ensues, followed probably by some hot words. In a few moments all the seats are occupied; the conductor rings his bell, and the car starts.

'At the Finsbury Pavement terminus of the North Metropolitan Tramways we find cars, nearly all carrying their maximum number of passengers, arriving in rapid succession from various northern suburbs. At the Hampstead Road and other termini north of the Thames they are arriving and departing every minute. Passing to South London we see further proofs of the great popularity of trams. The London County Council's cars, filled with almost every type of the great city's male and female workers, are following each other closely on their way to Blackfriars, Waterloo, or Westminster Bridge.

'Stand at the Elephant and Castle on a sunny afternoon. … In every direction heavily-laden trams and buses are passing each other. By you on the pavement is a line of 'bus and tram timekeepers, every one of them busily making notes in a bulgy pocket-book with a stumpy lead pencil.

'During the afternoon the trams carry comparatively few passengers, but at six p.m. they begin to fill up rapidly at every town-end terminus, including those of the electric cars at Hammersmith and Shepherd's Bush, and struggles to get on them are fierce and frequent. At ten o'clock the trams begin to pass into the yards; at long intervals at first, but after eleven o'clock every two or three minutes. Here is a late one entering the South London Tramway Company's big yard at Clapham Junction. A stableman is awaiting it, and the moment it stops he promptly takes out the horses, and leads them upstairs to unharness, feed, and make them secure for the night. As the horses are being led away, the driver and the conductor put their shoulders to the car and push it along the lines until it is close against the one in front of it. The driver then marches off home, with his rug on his arm and his whip in his hand. The conductor, however, is not quite ready to depart; for two or three minutes he sits inside the car checking his last journey's takings. Having made his money agree with his way bill, he enters the little yard-office and hands it in, together with his unused tickets, to the night inspector.

'The last tram has entered one of the London County Council's yards, the gates are shut, and the washers and stablemen are left to themselves. The washers vigorously sweep the dirt and the "dead" tickets from the roofs and insides of the cars, and not until this task is ended is the washing begun. It is nearly five o'clock before the last car is washed, but the washers' work is not yet finished — the windows have to be cleaned, the brass work polished, and the panels rubbed with chamois leather.'

London's horse tramways had another advantage: they provided 'test tracks' for the various forms of mechanical and electrical tramway haulage that were developed in the 1880s and early 1890s. These trials included:

- 4 March 1882 — a battery-electric tramcar on the North Metropolitan Tramways' Stratford–Leytonstone route;
- 10 March 1883 — an Anthony Rexkenzaun-designed battery-electric tramcar on the West Metropolitan Tramways, north of Kew Bridge;
- February 1885 — a battery-electric tramcar on the South London Tramways in Queen's Road, Battersea;

- September 1885 — a Jarman battery tramcar between Blackfriars and Clapham;
- 1885 — steam operation on the North London Tramways (to 1891);
- 1892/3 — an internal-combustion-engined tram — The Connelly Motor — on the London, Deptford & Greenwich Tramways.

London's horse-tramway period also saw the construction of two cable tramways. First was the Highgate Hill cable tramway, the first in Europe, which opened on 29 May 1884 and operated until 24 August 1909; the second was the Kennington–Streatham cable tramway, which opened on 7 December 1892 and operated until 15 April 1904. Both lines were taken over by the LCC and converted to electric traction, but not without some difficulty, as will be seen later.

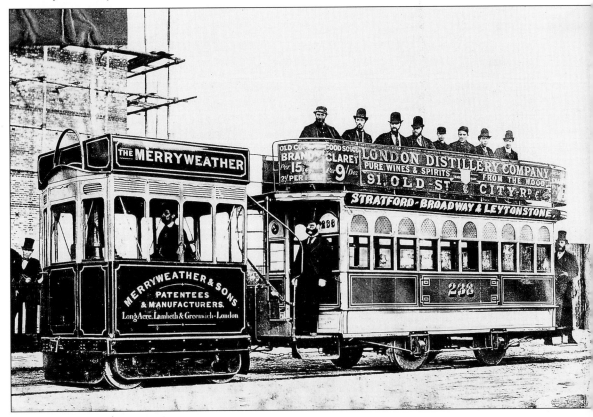

Eight years before regular steam traction began on the North Metropolitan Tramway in 1885 a trial was conducted in 1877 using a locomotive supplied by Merryweather & Sons. This was tried on the Stratford–Leytonstone line towing North Met horse car No 238. *National Tramway Museum*

Left: The Highgate Hill cable tramway was the first in Europe. It opened on 29 May 1884 and operated until 24 August 1909. The line was only short — 7/10 mile — but had the unusual feature of allowing a limited number of seats in the gripper car, in this case No 6. *IAL*

Centre left: In 1892/3 an internal-combustion-engined tram — 'The Connelly Motor' — was tried for six months on the London, Deptford & Greenwich Tramways. Built by Weymann of Guildford, it had a two-cylinder engine that ran on naphtha, developing 12-13hp. *National Tramway Museum*

Below left: After taking over the Kennington–Streatham cable tramway (opened on 7 December 1892), on 1 January 1899, the LCC modified the line's trailer cars to include cable gripper apparatus. One such car is seen here in 1899, shortly after conversion. After descending the hill horses would be attached and the cars would continue to Kennington. The line remained in operation until 15 April 1904. *National Tramway Museum*

Above right: The North Metropolitan Tramway operated the largest horse tramway in London. Here, at the Archway Tavern, cars, horses, drivers and conductors pose for the camera before working the Angel and Moorgate routes. *IAL*

Right: One of London's busy street corners — King's Cross — with omnibus and tramway traffic much in evidence. Above the tramcar is an impressive telegraph array atop Rickett, Smith & Co. *Author's collection*

Above: Washing LCC horse trams at the end of a day's duty, c1902. The car numbers give an indication of the size of the fleet. *Author's collection*

Below: Another LCC depot scene, this time from 1903. Car 124 has come off duty and the horses are being led away to their stabling. If the above account is to be believed, the driver and the conductor would then have put their shoulders to the car, and pushed it along the lines until it was close against the one in front of it. *National Tramway Museum*

Above: LCC horse car No 228 working a modified route to Holborn. The change was probably part of the LCC's ongoing electrification programme, which did not affect services running to the Nag's Head until July 1908. *Author's collection*

Below: London's last horse tramway was the LCC's Bricklayer's Arms–Rotherhithe line. It was closed on 30 April 1915 as an economy measure during the Great War, and the line was not reopened or electrified. *National Tramway Museum*

3. '…such a metallic network overhead' — The LCC electrification

London's tramway history until the late 1880s — lots of individual companies with their own territories and little co-ordination — was a reflection of its local government. Retrospectively, it is perhaps surprising that up to this period London did not have a single authority responsible for its growth and development; much power still rested with boards of guardians, parishes and vestry committees, plus three county councils. The city's one overriding authority, the Metropolitan Board of Works, had also largely discharged (sic) its duty in completing Sir Joseph Bazalgette's major drainage scheme for the city.

Growing demand for public transport in a city with an ever expanding population was just one of many pressures that led to the formation of the County of London under the terms of the Local Government Act 1888, creating a new administrative area. Most of London was in Middlesex, but the new authority also took in parts of Surrey and Kent. The area included 28 separate boroughs, plus the City Corporation, responsible for the financial centre of the city.

The new London County Council came into being on 1 April 1889. It assumed the functions of the Metropolitan Board of Works and many of those formerly discharged by the various local boards and committees. It did not take long for someone within the new Council to realise that it had acquired the power of compulsory purchase over the tramways in its area, and that this could be exercised after 21 years from the date of authorisation of their construction. With the first tramways having opened in 1870, that time was near.

On 12 November 1891 the LCC served notice on the London Street Tramways Co that it intended to purchase compulsorily part of its system that now qualified under Section 43 of the Tramways Act 1870, but it soon realised the folly of such a piecemeal approach and deferred further attempts until whole companies became available for purchase. Thus on 24 June 1896 the LCC acquired the lines of the North Metropolitan Tramways Co within the county, plus the whole of the London Street Tramways Co, but, lacking any powers to operate tramways, these were leased back to the North Metropolitan to work them. Powers to act as a tramway operator were acquired later in 1896, and between then and 24 August 1909 the LCC acquired nine other tramway companies, in whole or part, at a cost of £2,408,845 for 105¼ street-miles of lines.

By the late 1890s it was clear that the future of tramways lay in electric traction. To advise it on the best system to adopt, the LCC engaged Prof Alexander Kennedy, a leading electrical engineer. His brief was to report:

a) as to the best system or systems of mechanical traction, other than steam or cable, for adoption on the tramways;

b) where, or under what conditions, an experimental line could best be introduced to initiate such a system or systems; and

c) generally on the whole subject.

Prof Kennedy reported back on 5 June 1899. He had looked at gas and compressed air trams but found that: 'if they could be successfully carried out they would certainly have the advantage that the cars would be self-contained and independent of each other or of any overhead or underground work. … Unfortunately, neither of them has attained sufficient success to warrant me in recommending their use on London tramways.'

Of electrical systems, Prof Kennedy had looked at overhead, underground-conduit or - slot, surface-contact and battery systems. He found the overhead system to be 'by far the most used', and not to require 'any special interference with the roadway', but objected to it because 'at crossing at street junctions … the trolley system is accompanied by such a metallic network overhead as in my opinion to put it altogether out of the question in busy London streets'. With great foresight he also saw 'no engineering difficulty whatever in using a mixed tramway system, i.e. partly underground and partly overhead'.

Of conduit systems, Prof Kennedy found that 'the laying out and working of lines on a slot system has already been carried out on a very large scale', but that 'any underground system will cost considerably more per mile than even a first-class overhead line'. Nonetheless, he felt that the system's use of insulated conductors throughout, not using the rails as a return, reduced 'the possibility of electrolysis due to leakage currents and the disturbance of telegraphs and telephones'.

Prof Kennedy found that surface-contact systems combined the best features of the above, in having no overhead wires, but were cheaper to construct than conduit lines. Against them was the use of the rails for current return and the fact that 'in our moist climate … the working of the system depends on the permanence of a very large number (from 300 to 1,500 per mile of single line) of coils of fine wire placed in switchboxes or in separate chambers underground or along the line'. Finally, he dismissed batteries on the grounds that they 'add very greatly to the weight of the car (from 2½ to 4½ tons), their maintenance is very considerable, and they are practically only suitable for use on level lines'.

Overall, Prof Kennedy found that 'the London County Council ought to adopt, over all the central parts of their lines, an underground system — that is to say, a system in which overhead wires are entirely dispensed with.' He also recommended an experimental line 'of five or six miles', and monitoring of 'the proposal of a private company [London United Tramways] to bring a portion of their overhead lines within the county of London'. In his final comment, Prof Kennedy remarked that 'if it should be decided to carry out the long extensions to the south of London on an overhead system, there is no difficulty in arranging the cars so that they

can run from underground to overhead either with no stoppage at all … or with stoppage of only a few seconds.'

Prof Kennedy's report was adopted by the LCC, and on 17 October 1899 he was engaged as 'engineer in charge of the work of applying mechanical traction to an experimental line of tramway from Westminster Bridge to Lower Tooting'.

As plans for this experimental line were prepared, Londoners had an opportunity to see their tramway of the future at the International Tramways and Light Railways Exhibition, held at the Royal Agricultural Hall, Islington between 25 June and 4 July 1900. All they had to do was to visit the British Westinghouse Electric & Manufacturing Co's exhibit:

'Anybody who may heretofore have doubted the immense superiority of the electric tramway over the old fashioned "bus" which still plays so important a part in the streets of London, would have his doubts dispelled if, after reaching the Agricultural Hall in one of the ordinary conveyances, he had taken a short ride through the building on the elegant Westinghouse tramcar, and looked into the method of propelling and guiding the modern vehicle. The Westinghouse exhibit was in fact a complete and convincing answer to the question as to whether the adoption of electrical locomotion will furnish the means of traffic that the inhabitants of the metropolis require, and will really inaugurate a new era of "domestic locomotion". Visitors pausing before the splendid array of the products of the British Westinghouse Electric and Manufacturing Company could see almost at a glance the whole system of working an electric railway from the power-house to the moving car.

'The track on which the car was running had a continuous length of 310 feet, extending over the full length of the hall, and was left open for inspection, excepting for a short stretch on either end, paved with wooden blocks, which served to show the appearance that the track has in a real street. As seen through the open portion, the line in the Exhibition, in perfect imitation of a real line of the Westinghouse conduit system, consisted of a series of cast-iron yokes, each cast in one piece, and carefully strengthened by ribs at points where the greatest strain is likely to occur. These yokes, spaced five feet apart, centre to centre, bear the tramrails at their extremities, with the channel rails, conduit. section, and automatic switches which characterise the Westinghouse type of line, in the centre. The Westinghouse conduit system is free from all objections urged against the trolley system and is not only reliable, but safe; for in actual practice the conduit, extending between the yokes, is of concrete and encloses two conductors, one for the supply and the other for the return current, and, the current cannot run astray and do mischief by corroding gas or water pipes as is the case where other systems exist. Both the lead and the return conductors are isolated from the yokes and earth by means of porcelain insulators fixed to the yokes at suitable points of the track, and the car picks up the current from one conductor and returns it by the other, by means of a so-called contact "plough" which is connected to the car by a suitable insulated connection passing through a narrow open slot.

'How smoothly and accurately the whole system works was noticed by all visitors to the Exhibition and most of them no doubt formulated the wish to see it in practical operation in the metropolis and the suburbs.'

The LCC was also clearly impressed by the Westinghouse exhibit, because it bought it, and laid it down around its depot at Camberwell. This allowed familiarisation with the technology, and Prof Kennedy an opportunity to make alterations to the slot rail. Once satisfied with the results, the LCC held an open day at Camberwell, on 14 February 1901, to which members of the various borough councils were invited. A short demonstration track had been laid down, upon which the Westinghouse car, eventually to become No 101 in the LCC fleet, ran. There was also an exposed curved section of track:

'Owing to the impossibility of getting more than a few yards of track rail and slot rail, the track actually shown was not exactly that which is really to be used. The slot rail exposed a much greater surface of metal in the road than is shown in the design submitted to the Board of Trade. ... It also applied to the conductor tees, which are of greater depth than those proposed, and therefore lie nearer to the yokes than they actually should. ... it is hoped that the first part of the Council's tramways will be reconstructed and be worked by electrical traction about eighteen months from this date.'

This was not to be.

Electrification of the LCC Tramways was in part delayed by the Council's insistence upon being its own power supplier, and to that end it was building its own station at Greenwich, which would not be ready before the tramways were completed. Therefore, on 9 July 1901, the LCC resolved to go into partnership with the South London Electricity Supply Corporation, which was registered on

An overall view of the British Westinghouse conduit exhibit at the International Tramways and Light Railways Exhibition, held at the Royal Agricultural Hall, Islington between 25 June and 4 July 1900. *IAL*

Above: Close-up view of the British Westinghouse conduit exhibit at Islington, showing the control equipment (left) and a very heavily-loaded car. The raised track allowed the conduit plough to be seen as the car worked along. *IAL*

Right: The short section of conduit track laid down for inspection in Camberwell depot on 14 February 1901 by a visiting party from the London Boroughs. *IAL*

Below right: Westinghouse's former demonstration car was set up to run on a short length of conduit track inside Camberwell depot. Here it is on 14 February 1901, which looks to have been a cold day. *IAL*

4 December 1896 to supply electricity to Lambeth; its supply started on 28 November 1898.

On 5 November 1901, the LCC Highways Committee recommended acceptance of the tender of J. G. White & Co for 'the execution of the roadwork and plate laying required in connection with the reconstruction for electric traction of the Tramways between:

Westminster Bridge–Tooting
Blackfriars Bridge–Kennington
Waterloo Road–St George's'.

Total cost was £171,145.

On 24 April 1902 the LCC considered nine tenders for the supply of 100 double-deck, double-bogie tramcars. Prices varied from £65,880 to £83,500, and delivery times from 24 to 70 weeks. Again, the decision largely rested with Prof Kennedy, who recommended different suppliers for different components:

- Trucks — J. G. Brill Co, USA;
- Car bodies — Messrs Milnes and the Electric Railway & Carriage Works;
- Plough — Messrs J. G. White & Co.

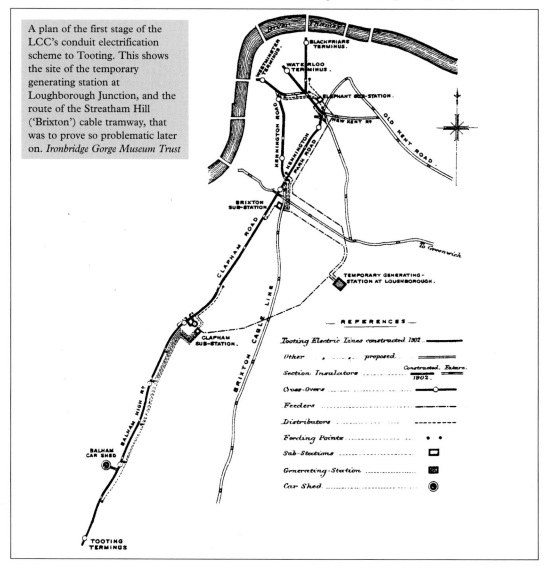

A plan of the first stage of the LCC's conduit electrification scheme to Tooting. This shows the site of the temporary generating station at Loughborough Junction, and the route of the Streatham Hill ('Brixton') cable tramway, that was to prove so problematic later on. *Ironbridge Gorge Museum Trust*

The two lowest tenders which allowed for these were:

- The British Thomson-Houston Co — £70,330, and
- Messrs Dick, Kerr & Co — £71,754.

Prof Kennedy, however, felt that Dick, Kerr & Co's motors 'are the most powerful and give better acceleration than any others', and he therefore considered them 'worth more than the difference in price, which amounts to about £7 per motor. Moreover that firm is prepared to deliver the whole of the 100 cars within twenty-four weeks ... instead of the thirty-six weeks specified by the other firm, and the difference in time is important, having regard to the desirability of the tramways being worked by electric traction at the earliest possible time.'

Costs were rocketing. In July 1902 a revised estimate for the LCC Tramways was put at £981,497. The increase of £357,997 (57%) was mainly due to the Greenwich power station.

By December 1902, between 500 and 600 men were at work on the electrification, and an average of 700ft of single line was completed per day, the most being 920ft. The first batch of 180 cars for the new conduit system was delivered by mid-April 1903, and a new order for 200 was placed. The double deck cars cost £659 and the smaller, single-truck cars cost £529. They were assembled and prepared for service at Marius Road depot, built for horse trams and situated off the Balham High Road.

Finally, by early-May 1903, the first section of the LCC's conduit tramway — between Westminster and Tooting — was ready for opening. This was performed by HRH The Prince of Wales (later King George V) on Friday 15 May 1903. Before the opening there was a seated banquet for 2,334 people held in a huge marquee erected in the grounds of the adjacent St Thomas's Hospital. After the banquet there were a number of speeches, to which the Prince of Wales replied:

'We are happy to have this opportunity of identifying ourselves with this great scheme, which will so materially benefit the working classes, in whose welfare we take the deepest interest. We and our two sons are looking forward with much pleasure to our journey from here to Tooting in the first electric car which will carry the public over the line. ... We do not wish to begin by defrauding the Council, we have therefore brought four halfpennies with which to pay for our tickets. ... I think that we are not dealing only with locomotion; it is also a question of health. By giving cheap facilities of access from the heart of the capital to the suburban districts you are removing the working classes from the scene of their daily toil, and from what are still too often insanitary dwellings, to healthy districts where light, air, and cheerful surroundings are obtainable.'

The Royal party was then led to one of the cars in Westminster Bridge Road: 'The car was painted white and festooned outside with evergreens. Inside the ordinary seats had not been fixed, and in their place were chairs upholstered in pale blue and white. The curtains were also blue and white, and the car was carpeted. The Prince and Princess took their seats inside the car, but the young Princes climbed to the top, where they were joined later by their father. Each of Their Royal Highnesses paid the halfpenny fare.' The Prince of Wales started the car off, but it was driven the rest of the way to Tooting by Alfred Baker, Manager of the LCC Tramways. Public services began the same evening, and were well patronised.

To effect the opening, the LCC was using a temporary generating station at Tooting, erected at Loughborough Junction, as its own power station at Greenwich was not ready. This 'temporary' station cost £74,000, and remained in use until 19 July 1906. Greenwich did not open formally until 26 May 1906. Its estimated cost was £900,000. It was built on Crowley's Wharf, on Hoskins Street and Old Woolwich Road.

As more and more electrified lines opened, the LCC began to dispose of its tram horses. A large sale was held on 9 March 1904 where 180 were sold. The highest price paid for a single horse was £89; the average price was £41.

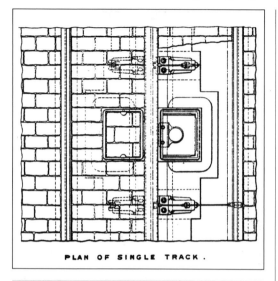

PLAN OF SINGLE TRACK.

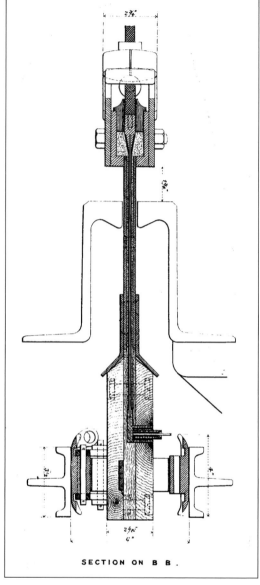

SECTION ON B B.

Above: Cross-section of the LCC's conduit track through a supporting yoke. The running rails and slot rails can be seen. Below the latter is the conduit slot, with its 'T' conductor rails.
Ironbridge Gorge Museum Trust

Right: An enlarged view of a conduit plough passing through the slot rails, and showing the spring-loaded conductors that maintained contact with the 'T' rails. *Ironbridge Gorge Museum Trust*

Below: Front and side elevations of a conduit plough mounted beneath a tramcar, showing the method of current collection by this system. On the early LCC tramcars the ploughs rode in a carrier that formed part of one of the bogie trucks.
Ironbridge Gorge Museum Trust

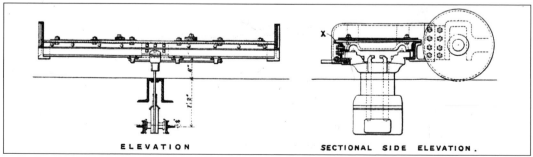

ELEVATION

SECTIONAL SIDE ELEVATION.

Above and right: Two views of construction work by J. G. White & Co on the LCC's Tooting line, showing the laying in of the yokes forming the conduit slot, and the installation of the slot rails above this. *IAL*

Below right: Later conduit construction in York Road, Wandsworth, in the middle of 1906, showing the depth of roadway that had to be dug out. Conduit pointwork was complicated by the need for the ploughs to move over with the tramcars. This trackwork came into use on 5 August 1906. *Author's collection*

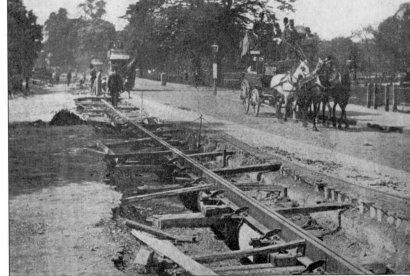

Above: Marius Road depot was a former horse-tram depot that was used to assemble the first 100 Class A LCC tramcars before they entered service in May 1903. It had four roads and was equipped with a traverser. Cars 22, 3, 37 and 4 can be seen awaiting service, whilst horse tram No 164 sits at the end of a side road. *Author's collection*

Below: An LCC 'A' class car, seen in original condition before 1906, when alterations were made to the stairs and top covers were fitted. The bogie plough carrier is seen to good advantage here. One hundred of these cars inaugurated the LCC's conduit tramway service in May 1903. *A. D. Packer Collection/National Tramway Museum*

Above: The public's first view of the new LCC trams came in the weeks leading up to the official opening of the lines, as cars travelled around as part of driver training. Car No 50 is seen at Balham railway bridge, and seems to have drawn a small crowd of onlookers.
National Tramway Museum

Right: The opening ceremony of the LCC Tramways at 3.30pm on 15 May 1903. Car No 86, painted in a special white with blue lining livery, is seen leaving Westminster Bridge Road with HRH The Prince of Wales at the controls. *IAL*

Below right: A line-up of the people responsible for the LCC Tramways electrification. Those depicted include Prof Alexander Kennedy (bearded), who is standing to the right of Alfred Baker, the General Manager of the LCC Tramways. *IAL*

Left: At Blackfriars terminus the LCC proposed to erect queue pens: 'There will be two starting places for the cars — one above and one below Stamford Street; each would have a narrow pen for each route served from the starting place, and each pen would contain a car load of people. The pens would be near the refuges now in the roadway. Men in uniform would be employed to keep people off the cars, which will have collapsible gates.' One of the queue pens is shown at Marius Road depot, with a somewhat self-conscious bunch of depot workers pretending to be passengers. Surely the pens were not to be used over the track like this? *IAL*

Below: Old and New trams at Catford — Class C car No 290 and horse tram No 338. The Class C cars were the first LCC ones to receive top covers, from 1904. That year also saw a number of sales of former tram horses — average price £41. *National Tramway Museum*

Above: East Dulwich station, c1908, with LCC
Class C car No 248. Through the railway bridge is
the foot of the notorious Dog Kennel Hill, which
required cars using it to be equipped with additional
brakes. On 6 May 1912 the LCC opened an
additional pair of tracks up this hill.
Author's collection

Below: The opening of the LCC Tramways route
across Blackfriars Bridge on 14 September 1909 was
the 59th opening since the original one in May
1903. The ceremony here was because this line,
which ran from Blackfriars to Southwark Bridge
Road via Blackfriars Bridge and Southwark Street,
included a stretch of track within the area of the City
Corporation of London, which, up to this date, had
been implacably opposed to tramways. *IAL*

4. Underground, overground — Private investment in London's tramways

As in many other towns and cities, London's tramways were largely developed by private companies. Unlike in many other towns and cities, in London three private companies retained a significant role in the development of the city's tramways throughout the period of electrification, and on into the early 1930s, in tandem with major investments by county and local authorities. Moreover, by 1913 the management of these three companies had become unified and tied in with that of London's major bus company and some of its underground railways. The formation of this combine created a major force in the development of tramways and other public transport in London, and was an important influence upon the later establishment and direction of the London Passenger Transport Board (LPTB).

London's first overhead electric tramway also owed its existence to a private company. As part of the planned reopening of Alexandra Palace and its Park Grounds in 1898, the new management allowed a German company —

Elektrizitätsgesellschaft Wandruszka of Berlin — to build an electric railway from the Park gates, by Wood Green station on the Great Northern Railway, to the Palace's east entrance, as a demonstration line for its products. The line was just under half a mile long and climbed at an average gradient of 1 in 13. It had standard-gauge track, but it was the four vehicles that worked the line that were of the greatest interest. They were in effect single-deck tramcars, electrically powered through overhead wires. Called the Alexandra Park Electric Railway, the line came into use on 13 May 1898 — five weeks after the Park's reopening. In its first season, until 5 November 1898, 172,000 passengers rode the cars. Only opening for a week at Christmas, Alexandra Palace and its Electric Railway reopened on 31 March 1899, but closed early on 30 September 1899 in deep financial trouble. The railway was sold to pay Wood Green UDC, a major creditor. A sad end for the line that gave Londoners a first taste of their tramway future.

One of the four cars of the Alexandra Park Electric Railway. They were built by the Waggonfabrik Falkenried in Hamburg. Despite the English notice, the photograph was taken in Germany before the cars were shipped to the UK. The 50-seater cars ran for only two seasons, between 13 May 1898 and 30 September 1899. *National Tramway Museum*

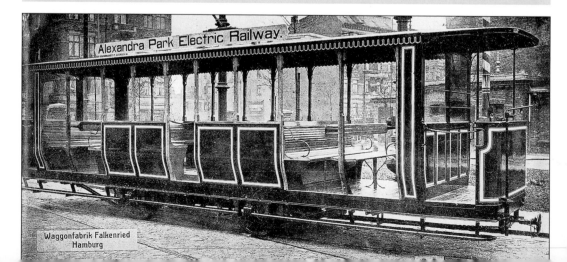

London United Tramways

The London United Tramways (LUT) developed just over 53 miles of electric tramways, mostly in the west of London, between the years 1901 and 1915. The company was formed on 19 July 1894, to acquire the assets of the bankrupt West Metropolitan Tramways Co Ltd from the receiver. Beginning with the acquisition of another failed venture — The Southall, Ealing & Shepherd's Bush Tram-Railway Co — on 12 August 1881, the West Metropolitan had built up a small network of lines from Shepherd's Bush to Kew Bridge and Hammersmith. On acquiring the West Metropolitan's assets in August 1894, the LUT's General Manager — James Clifton Robinson — set about making the run-down company work. Older, one-horse cars were scrapped, and the staff put into uniforms, but Robinson's real ambitions lay elsewhere. He wanted to electrify the tramways using the overhead-trolley system, and to expand the network.

A charismatic and persuasive person, James Robinson garnered the support of most of the local authorities and committees through whose areas the lines passed, but he met solid resistance to overhead wires from the LCC. To get around this, lines were planned which lay mostly outside LCC jurisdiction. A Bill for the electrification and extension of the LUT's tramways was placed before Parliament in 1898, but some of the proposed lines were removed in the Parliamentary process, and it was a trimmed and amended Bill which became law on 2 August 1898.

Construction work on the LUT's first electric line started in Brentford on 20 March 1899 and they were all substantially completed by June 1900, but their opening was delayed by objections over electrical insulation from Greenwich and Kew observatories. These doubts also embraced those underground railways which were embarking upon electrification at the same time, and the situation was deemed sufficiently serious for a conference of all interested parties to be held in October 1899. No agreement was forthcoming, and the LUT's tramway remained horse-worked, with its electric cars locked away in Chiswick, next to an idle power station. An *impasse*, from out of which a way had to be found, because 'the opinion of practical men [was] that it was not the observation of sunspots, but the convenience

Right: One of the one-horse former West Metropolitan Tramways cars James Robinson scrapped when the LUT took control of the undertaking in August 1894. The car is on the Shepherd's Bush Green–Young's Corner service.
National Tramway Museum

Below right: The LUT renovated the best of the West Metropolitan Tramways two-horse cars when it took over in 1894. This view shows one such car at the old Kew Bridge on the Hammersmith route. *National Tramway Museum*

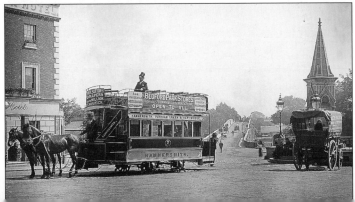

of 5,000,000 people in London that was at stake'. Eventually, on 3 April 1901, HM Treasury agreed to pay £10,000 for the removal of the Kew Observatory to Eskdalemuir in Dumfries-shire, and at 7.00am on 4 April 1901 the LUT opened its Shepherd's Bush–Acton Hill, Shepherd's Bush–Kew Bridge via Goldhawk Road, and Hammersmith Broadway–Young's Corner, Chiswick lines, the day being declared 'a memorable day in the story of London tramway enterprise'.

On 6 July 1901 the LUT opened its Kew Bridge–Hounslow line and on 10 July formally opened the whole system, plus a new line between Acton and Southall. Finally, opinion could be expressed upon what the company had achieved:

'At Shepherd's Bush is the terminus of the Central London Railway — the "Twopenny Tube". On the opening of the electric tramway, starting from that terminus to Kew, Acton, etc., quite a remarkable demonstration of the value of electric traction was brought to the knowledge of London. It was found that a delightful holiday in one of London's choicest public resorts, Kew Gardens, could be enjoyed for the sum of 8d! This was the object lesson which the directors of this company had long desired to bring before the minds of the people of London, and the

Left: With the end of the wait in sight, on 5 February 1901 the LUT made trial trips with some of its 'mothballed' fleet, including 'Z' class No 90, whose smartly-turned-out crew are keen to get on with things as they prepare to depart Chiswick depot. *IAL*

Below left: A view of the formal opening of the LUT on 10 July 1901, declared 'a memorable day in the story of London tramway enterprise'. Festooned with garlands, and loaded with men in top hats, the cars lead off in procession.
National Tramway Museum

Right: Shepherd's Bush terminus of the LUT in July 1901, showing its proximity to the terminus of the Central London Railway (left). 'From the Bank ... to Shepherd's Bush costs 2d. At the exit from the underground electric line are found the splendid cars of the London United Tramways, conveying the passenger to Kew Bridge for another 2d.' *IAL*

phenomenal success of the lines on the great public holidays has demonstrated how thoroughly the public has learned the lesson. From the Bank … to Shepherd's Bush costs 2d. At the exit from the underground electric line are found the splendid cars of the London United Tramways, conveying the passenger to Kew Bridge for another 2d., the whole journey occupying considerably under one hour. The return occupies the same time and costs the same sum, so that for 8d. an inhabitant of London discovered he could enjoy a double journey of about 12 miles, occupying less than two hours, with a whole day in Kew Gardens. In place of one train an hour there is a "Tube" train every three minutes, and electric cars at the terminus thereof, supplying a constant service of three minute, two minute and even *one* minute intervals, when necessary, to meet the public demand.'

The LUT system grew with the addition of new lines until 1907:

8 November 1902	Hampton Court via Hampton Wick
13 August 1903	Hounslow–Hounslow Heath and Isleworth–Twickenham
4 April 1903	Hampton Court via Hampton
1 June 1904	Hammersmith–Uxbridge via Acton
1 March 1906	Hampton Wick–Surbiton and Surbiton–Tolworth
26 May 1906	Brentford–Hanwell and Kingston Hill–Malden
27 April 1907	Malden–Raynes Park
2 May 1907	Raynes Park–Wimbledon Broadway
27 June 1907	Wimbledon Hill Road–Merton and Haydon's Road–'The Plough'

James Robinson was knighted in 1905. Sadly, however, he collapsed on a New York tramcar on 6 November 1910, and died shortly afterwards.

On 20 November 1912 a company called the London & Suburban Traction Co Ltd was formed by BET and the London Underground Railways Group to run the LUT, BET's MET and, ultimately, the SMET, and on 1 January 1913 the London & Suburban Traction Co took control of both the LUT and MET, with the SMET following suit in June 1913. In addition to its tube-railway interests, from January 1912 the London General Omnibus Co (LGOC) had also been a member of the London Underground Railways Group. At the end of July 1915, the LUT opened its last extension, of its Acton terminus by 159yd, to join up with MET lines.

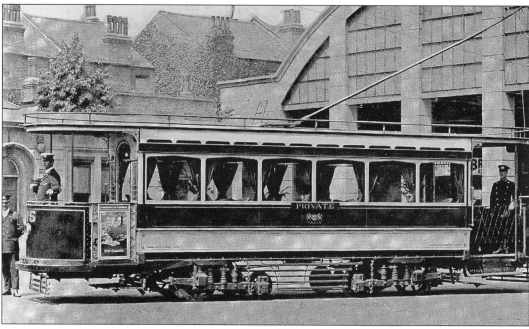

Left: A view of the LUT's headquarters at 74 High Road, Chiswick. Apart from a bicycle and a carriage, the trams have the road to themselves! *IAL*

Below left: Perks of the job? Car No 175 was termed a 'Luxury Saloon' and, when not on hire, was kept in a private siding at Garrick Villa — James Robinson's home at Hampton — which came into use on 1 March 1906. *IAL*

Above right: The LUT also opened three new routes on 1 March 1906, including one between High Street, Hampton Wick, and Winters Bridge, that crossed Kingston Bridge. This local commemorative postcard recorded the first car — No 320 — to cross the bridge. *National Tramway Museum*

Right: Before the introduction of its modern tramcars in the early 1930s, in the mid-1920s the LUT modernised its ageing fleet. Class T car No 327 of 1906 was reconditioned in 1925, receiving high-powered motors and magnetic brakes. *IAL*

Metropolitan Electric Tramways

The Metropolitan Electric Tramways Co Ltd was the largest of the three private companies operating electric tramways in London. Its track mileage — at just over 53 miles — was nearly identical with that of the LUT, but it ultimately came to own and operate more cars. It developed electric tramways, mostly in the north and northwest of London, between 1904 and 1911, but unlike the LUT did not own many of the lines, 38¼ miles being leased from Middlesex and Hertfordshire county councils.

The Metropolitan Tramways & Omnibus Co Ltd was formed in 1894, but on 1 October 1901 its name was changed to the simpler Metropolitan Electric Tramways Co Ltd (MET), and the company became a wholly-owned subsidiary of BET. By a share-exchange arrangement, the MET came to own 75% of the North Metropolitan Tramways Co, which it set about trying to electrify. The company's first electric line — Wood Green–Haringey–Finsbury Park — opened on 22 July 1904, and was followed by 40 more lines up to and including Ponders End–Enfield, the company's last, on 20 February 1911.

On 1 January 1913 the London & Suburban Traction Co Ltd took control of MET.

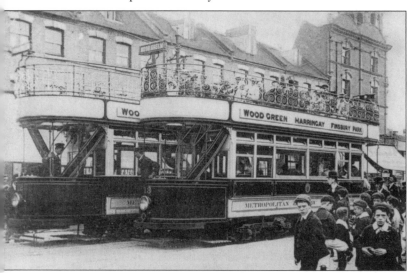

Left: Opening day for the MET on 22 July 1904, with the inauguration of the company's first electric service: Wood Green–Harringay–Finsbury Park. 'B' type cars Nos 12 and 13 seem to be of less interest than the cameraman.
National Tramway Museum

Below: The Board of Trade inspection of the MET's Highgate–Whetstone line, its tenth, took place on 30 May 1905. 'A' type cars Nos 111 and 123 are to view, and by the latter there seems to be a large pile of setts still to be laid.
National Tramway Museum

Right: Opening day for the Highgate–Whetstone line was 5 June 1905. 'A' type car No 112 is seen at the Highgate terminus, directly under Highgate Archway, on the opening day. The significance of this location was that the boundary with London ran directly beneath the arch. *National Tramway Museum*

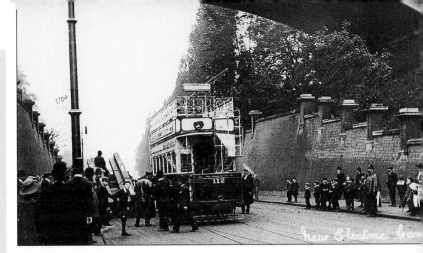

Centre right: On 11 April 1906 the MET opened a service to Alexandra Palace, which included the line of the Alexandra Park Electric Railway. Here the first car — No 145 — is seen working up to the Palace, with Mr E. G. Cole, Chairman of the Trustees, at the controls. *National Tramway Museum*

Below: Connections with the Alexandra Palace line were improved from 10 October 1906 when a service of double-deck cars from Finsbury Park was inaugurated. Passengers changed to Alexandra Palace cars here at Priory Road, Muswell Hill. The conductor on the car at right is swinging the trolley pole from the top deck! *National Tramway Museum*

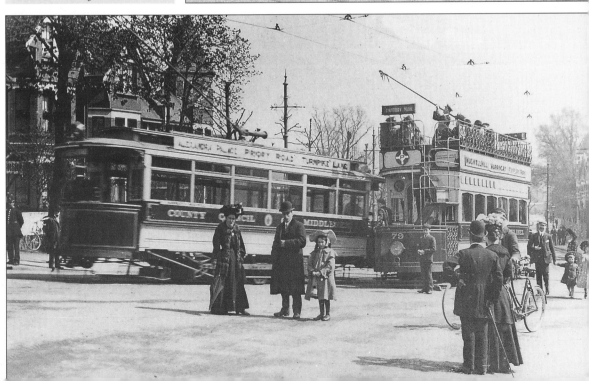

Left: MET cars reached Enfield on 1 July 1909. Car No 109 carried the official party that day. It was driven by Alderman Henry Burt, Chairman of Middlesex County Council Light Railways & Tramways Committee. *National Tramway Museum*

Below: Through-working over the LCC conduit lines by MET cars along the Great North Road finally came about on 24 September 1914, when this change pit in Archway Road, by the famous Tavern, came into use. A plough is seen being inserted under 'C/1' type car No 199 there on 14 September 1929. *National Tramway Museum*

The South Metropolitan Tramways & Electric Lighting Co Ltd

Smallest of the three private tramway companies was the South Metropolitan Tramways & Electric Lighting Co Ltd (SMET). The company was originally registered in 1899, but took this name in August 1904. It was another off-shoot of BET. The SMET developed just over 13 miles of electric tramways, mostly in the south of London, around Croydon, all of which came into use during 1906.

In building its lines, the SMET was particularly keen to rebut accusations that tramways spoil a district or lead to a depreciation in property values, and recited a series of improvements it had made in the course of its work:

- Ellis Davis House, Croydon — a number of houses demolished, and fine new thoroughfare made;
- Boundary Road — £40,000 spent on demolishing a narrow accommodation bridge over the railway and erecting in its place a new bridge 50ft wide;
- Park Lane, Carshalton — a width of 10ft added to a previously-rough country lane for a distance of 523yd;
- Ruskin Road — an entirely-new thoroughfare, 697yd long and 50ft wide, constructed between Park Lane and Carshalton Park Road;

- Rotherfield, Seymour and Cator Roads — three more new roads, each about 200ft long, leading into Ruskin Road and giving ready access to the tramways from the centre of Carshalton;
- Carshalton Road, opposite Windsor Castle Hotel — a roadway of only 17ft width increased to a width of between 32ft and 48ft following the company's purchase of land from a convent, demolition of a brick wall and felling of trees.

The first section of the SMET — to Penge — opened on 10 February 1906, with the remainder following later in the year:

12 April 1906	Pawleyne Arms–Thicket Road Robin Hood–Crystal Palace Low Level station
26 May 1906	Croydon (Canterbury Road)–Tooting
9 August 1906	West Croydon–Canterbury Road
10 November 1906	West Croydon–Carshalton (Windsor Castle Hotel)
21 December 1906	Depot–Sutton (Grapes)
24 June 1907	West Croydon–Crystal Palace (through-running agreement with Croydon Corporation)

On 14 June 1913 the London & Suburban Traction Co Ltd took control of the SMET.

Laying tramway lines in Carshalton Road, opposite the Windsor Castle Hotel. To the right can be seen the land SMET purchased from a nearby convent; the company then pulled down a brick wall, felled trees and widened the road to a width of between 32ft and 48ft.
National Tramway Museum

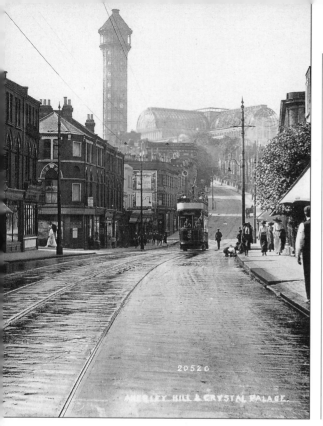

20520

ANERLEY HILL & CRYSTAL PALACE.

Left: Through a running agreement, on 24 June 1907 Croydon Corporation began a service between West Croydon and Penge, over company lines, and the SMET began a service from West Croydon-Crystal Palace over Corporation lines. Here, Corporation car No 30 has descended the worst of Anerley Hill down from the Crystal Palace, which dominates the horizon. *National Tramway Museum*

Below: In 1928 the Underground Group remodelled some of the SMET cars. This is the 'before' picture of 'J' class car No 16. At each end of the top decks were the 'Spencer Hoops', named after the General Manager of the Underground Tramways, Christopher Spencer, who had them fitted to prevent the trolley pole striking passengers when the cars passed beneath low bridges. *IAL*

Right: The interior of the same car, before its remodelling in at Hendon Works in 1928. *IAL*

Below right: This is 'J' class car No 16 after remodelling by the Underground Group in 1928. The lower saloon now has five windows, for increased strength, and the wooden body has had flush steel panels added. Inside, the longitudinal seating has been replaced by cross seats. *IAL*

5. '1,200 electric glowlights of varied colours' — Electric tramways in the London County Boroughs

On its formation in 1889 the County of London comprised 28 metropolitan boroughs whose tramways came to be provided by the LCC. In contrast, outlying county boroughs had largely to make their own arrangements with regard to tramways. Of the 10 such boroughs which eventually had electric tramways of their own, only three — Croydon, West Ham and Leyton — had been served by horse trams, having acquired the privately-operated tramways in their respective areas.

Croydon's first tramway route — North End–Thornton Heath Pond — was opened on 9 October 1879, and by 1883 the Croydon & Norwood Tramways Co was working four routes. By 1898 the tramways were in a poor state of repair; the Council therefore decided to exercise its powers under the Tramways Act 1870 and began to purchase the lines as each became eligible under the 21-year rule. By 1 January 1900 the purchase was completed, and the Corporation leased the tramways to the British Electric Traction Co Ltd (BET), which had approached it with a view to leasing the undertaking once this had been electrified.

Agreement was reached, and BET took over operation of the system until 1 June 1906.

Meanwhile, the tramways were being reconstructed for electric traction. Croydon's Tramways Committee reported its estimates for this work to the full Council on 24 September 1900:

Reconstruction of track and paving	£102,000
Overhead equipment	20,045
Feeders, test wires and road work	12,963
Cars	9,670
Motor car equipment	13,052
Excavating and guard wires	1,400
Thornton Heath car shed additions	4,700
Brighton Road car shed	4,700
Engineer's commission	3,000
Contingencies	5,000
Total	£176,530

Added to this was £50,000 for the purchase of the tramway company, making a grand total of just under £¼ million.

The first line came into operation on

Left: Relaying the track for electrification in central Croydon in 1900. The old building in the centre is Whitgift Hospital, which was completed in 1599. In the year 2000, Croydon Tramlink trams cross right–left along George Street, past the Hospital. *IAL*

Right: Croydon car No 21 seen just after the opening of the electric tramway in late September 1901. The tramway was operated by BET until 1 June 1906. *IAL*

26 September 1901, and the opening was attended with due ceremony. Press coverage was fulsome:

'The cars are handsome. There are to be thirty-five of them when the whole system is in working order. They are double decked and each car will seat fifty-two passengers. They are fitted with staircases of the reversed pattern. The seats on the top are of the garden type with reversible backs. The seats inside are of perforated bent-wood, and are not upholstered. Every car is equipped with two motors of 35 horse-power each. The cars are provided with two brakes, a powerful hand brake and also an electric emergency brake; this latter will, when the cars are travelling at full speed, bring them to a standstill in about eighteen yards on the level. ... The cars will only stop to set down and take up passengers at fixed points, which are indicated by bands painted on the trolley poles. At "compulsory" stopping places a broad white band is painted on the trolley pole with a red band painted on the white one. At these points the cars will always stop as a matter of course. "Voluntary" stopping places are indicated by a broad white band only, and the cars will stop at these points, if required, to put down or take up passengers. A large number of stopping places have been provided, the greatest distance a passenger will have to walk being about 150 yards.'

On 31 July 1909 the LCC inaugurated a through service to Norbury, its tracks coming to within feet of Croydon Corporation's, but this gap remained until late in 1925! Through-running of LCC cars into Croydon began on 7 February 1926. Upon absorption into the LPTB in 1933, Croydon Corporation contributed over 9¼ miles of track and 55 tramcars.

The largest of London's county boroughs was West Ham. In 1901 it was said of the borough that: 'No portions of Greater London have grown with more rapidity than West Ham, and the march of bricks and mortar is now extending many miles into the formerly agricultural district

Left: Through-running of LCC trams required the re-laying of some of the Croydon system to withstand the weight of their heavier cars. In 1925 a temporary passing loop was laid on the surface of London Road, Norbury, while the other track was re-laid for the LCC cars. Croydon car No 64 works away from the camera. The 'P' is a headlamp mask fitted during the Great War in response to blackout restrictions — it denoted a car going to Purley. *IAL*

Below left: In later years many ex-Croydon trams remained on local routes, notably the 42 to Thornton Heath, which was wholly within the borough. LPTB No 399 had been Croydon No 55, the last in its class of 'E/1' cars built in 1928. *V. C. Jones/IAL*

of South Essex. West Ham itself, which is the eighth largest municipality in the country, has increased its population within half a century from 18,817 to 267,308.'

West Ham acquired the horse tramways in its area in February 1903 and set about electrifying them. This task was delayed by an important legal case which had implications for all local authorities undertaking similar work. The local gas and water companies wanted their pipes moved from under the tramways, and to charge the Council for the work, but the latter refused. At arbitration the Board of Trade found for the Corporation, setting a valuable legal precedent.

The first electric tramway route in West Ham opened on 27 February 1904. On the formation of the LPTB the Corporation added just over 16 miles of track and 134 trams. Some ex-West Ham cars remained in operation until the very last day of tramway operation in London.

The last of the London Boroughs to open an electric tramway was Leyton, which did so on 1 December 1906, having purchased the horse tramways in its area on 1 November 1905. At a dinner to celebrate the opening, held at the Great Eastern Hotel, there were many toasts and speeches, but the tone was lightened considerably by the remarks of Mr F. W. Manders, a local contractor who had constructed the permanent way and the car sheds: 'Mr Manders showed the enormous quantity of material he had had to move (some 4,500 tons per week) with horses and carts in effecting the reconstruction of the track. He humorously observed that his contract contained

Right: A view in West Ham Lane shortly after the inauguration of West Ham Corporation's electric tramways in February 1904. The extraordinarily long side-arms were a feature of the system in its early days. *IAL*

Below: Some former West Ham trams remained in London Transport service until the end of tramway operation in July 1952. One was No 338, ex-West Ham No 132, of 1925, seen here on a special working in St George's Road on 25 May 1949. *V. C. Jones/IAL*

all sort of pains and penalties for any delays in finishing his work, but he had finished it two months ahead of the stipulated date, and, so far, had heard nothing of any bonus for having done so!'

Despite Mr Manders' best efforts, by the early 1920s Leyton's tramways had fallen into a sorry state, and they were taken over by the LCC for 10 years on 1 July 1921, this being renewed for a further 25 years in 1931.

The other London County Boroughs which had electric tramways were:

East Ham — opened 22 June 1901;
Ilford — opened 14 March 1903;
Bexley — opened 3 October 1903;
Barking — opened 1 December 1903, closed 16 February 1929;
Walthamstow — opened 3 June 1905;
Erith — opened 21 August 1905.

Left: The opening of Leyton District Council Tramways on 1 December 1906. Council Chairman A. W. Golightly drives away in the first of 10 decorated cars. Councillor Golightly's car had 1,200 electric 'glowlights' of varied colours on it, according to the account of the opening. *Author's collection*

Below: In 1930 Leyton District Council bought 50 new 'E/3' tramcars which were numbered in the LCC fleet but carried the town's coat of arms. These cars passed to the LPTB and some, like No 200, seen here on 5 May 1951, remained in service until the end of tramway operation in London. *V. C. Jones/IAL*

6. 'It is difficult to over-estimate the importance of this' — The Kingsway Subway

In the preface to a review of the progress of the LCC Tramways to 1909, the essential problem facing all of those who sought to provide such a service was summarised thus: 'They have to deal with the largest population in any city in the world. They have this population divided, approximately, into two halves by a river which is crossed by a limited number of bridges, over which the ordinary traffic is enormous and incessant. They have to meet the competition of surface and underground railways, as well as of motor and horsed omnibuses, and, moreover, in the very heart of the Metropolis there is an area of about one square mile, that is to say the City of London proper, within which tramways are not permitted to penetrate. Finally, the area over which the Council's tramways have to operate is greater, in relation to the density of the population, than that of any other large city.'

North-South communication by tramway across the city was a problem that bedevilled the LCC, and one to which it did not find an overall solution. The quest did, however, lead to one major innovation, and the construction of a feature unique to tramway operation in the UK.

By 1898, conditions in areas of unregulated housing around Holborn, next to the City of London proper, were so unsanitary that a decision was taken to clear them. The land thus opened up created an opportunity to use some of the new streets to be formed for tramways to link North and South London. At the same time it was also suggested that, if the trams were to run below these streets, in the manner recently adopted in New York, this would free the new thoroughfares for other traffic. A small deputation duly visited New York and Boston to see their subways at first hand. The party reported back to the LCC on 5 November 1901, and on 12 November the Council resolved to

seek powers for the construction of a subway for single-deck tramcars: 'The line was to commence at Theobald's Road, where it would form a junction with the existing tramway leased from the County Council. It would proceed along the level until Southampton Row was reached; then it would go below the level of the street in a subway varying in depth from 3ft to a little more, and pass along the site of the proposed new thoroughfare from Southampton Row to the Strand. There the line would turn towards the Embankment, which it would reach near Waterloo Bridge, where it would emerge into the open.'

The LCC sought powers to construct this subway in 1902, but the Bill came under concerted opposition from a number of vested interests. In Select Committee on 23-24 April 1902 the District Railway asked for a clause 'stopping the tramway before it debouches upon the Embankment', on the grounds that it would otherwise be laid over where their lines ran under, 'and the additional weight thus thrown upon the girders supporting the roof of the railway would involve great danger and serious injury'. A similar objection was posed by the Metropolitan Railway, whose lines also ran beneath at this point. When the LCC pointed out that 'no harm had hitherto resulted to the girders from the passage over the Embankment roadway of steam-rollers', the Metropolitan Railway's Engineer rejoined that 'steam-rollers did not run at twelve miles an hour'. However, with the addition of a few protective clauses, the Committee passed the Bill.

Both the subway and the streets beneath which it passed were constructed at the same time. A cross-section of the work at Kingsway shows that sewers and service-pipe conduits were constructed on either side of the subway so

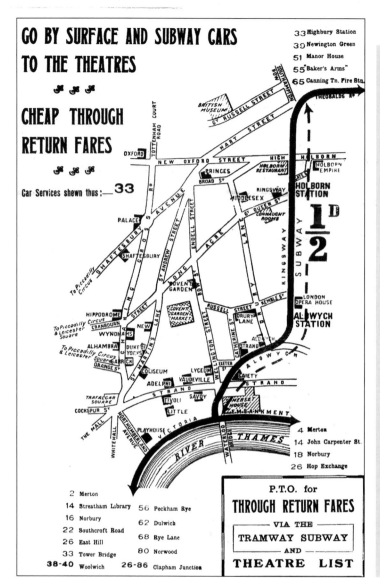

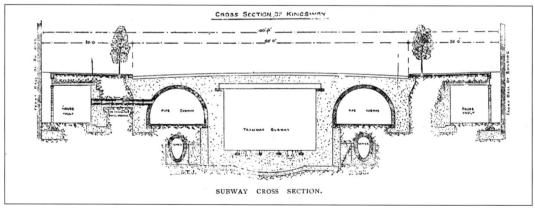

SUBWAY CROSS SECTION.

that 'it will never be necessary to break up the surface of Kingsway for the purpose of laying pipes'.

At first the LCC was unable to obtain Parliamentary sanction to purchase compulsorily the land and buildings it needed to build the subway beyond the Strand, and so the construction was divided into two stages, with that between Southampton Row and Aldwych starting first. The construction of the subway was of several kinds. The rails 'descend to below the surface in Southampton Row by a cutting in the centre of the street. The two lines are then carried in deep level cast-iron tubes under Holborn, and then rise to close to the surface at the station at Kingsway, a little to the north of Great Queen Street. From this point to the station, situated at the junction of Kingsway and Aldwych, the subway is close to the surface of the street … only about 3ft. After turning under the western arm of Aldwych, the subway falls very quickly again, so as to pass under the Strand, it continues along Wellington Street, the rails being 33ft below the surface, and finally emerges on the Embankment at road level.'

That was what was supposed to happen, but, although the subway was completed to Aldwych by June 1904, the LCC had still not obtained the powers necessary to extend it southwards, and there was also no tramway to connect with it. In order to get at least part of the subway open, a new tramway was laid down by rebuilding the North Metropolitan Tramways line along Theobalds Road, from the north entrance to the subway, which was then continued by a new line up Rosebury Avenue and St John Street to The Angel, Islington. Work began on this on 17 September 1905 and was completed quickly, as it came into use for driver training on 30 December 1905.

To work the new subway service, new tramcars were designed by Aubrey Fell and built by the United Electric Car Co Ltd at Preston. To comply with Board of Trade regulations for the construction of cars for tube railways, the trams had to be made entirely of non-flammable materials. They were mostly made from steel:

'The floors are constructed of steel plates, on the upper surface of which there is a covering of "Litosilo", and are again covered with wearing slats of non-flammable material. The seats are of the longitudinal type, and are formed of oak slats fixed to angle steel supports. The oak and all timber used in the cars is rendered non-flammable by a special process. Special care has been exercised in the design to provide efficient ventilation. Ventilators are arranged the full length of the clerestory to open simultaneously. By this means the air is driven into the car from the front end and expelled at the other. The inside finish of the cars is composed entirely of aluminium, on which suitable designs are chased and picked out in colours.'

Sixteen of these cars were ordered. They were known as Class F and numbered 552-567 in the LCC fleet. In October 1905, 34 more cars were ordered, this time from the Brush Electrical Engineering Co. Detail and equipment differences led to these cars being known as Class G; they took Nos 568-601.

The completed first section of the subway, together with the tramway connecting to the northern part of the LCC system, was available for driver training from 2 January 1906, and it was ceremonially opened by HM King Edward VII on 24 February 1906. Accounts of the opening put the cost to date at between £145,000 and £279,000, the latter being close to the original estimate of £282,000 for the whole subway scheme.

Later in 1906 the LCC finally obtained the permission it needed to complete the subway and to lay down the lines it was to connect to along the Embankment. In the meantime, the new service was proving a great success. Average takings on each car were 2s 2¼d per car mile, compared with an average of 1s per car mile on services south of the Thames. By 16 November 1906 the subway line extended above ground from The Angel a distance of two miles to the Archway Tavern, and on 14 December 1906 the new lines over Westminster Bridge and along Victoria Embankment were opened.

Work on the subway south of the Strand commenced on 11 March 1907. The work involved the construction of the two cast-iron tubes carrying the lines under the Strand, but it encountered its greatest difficulty beneath Wellington Street, between there and Waterloo

Left: The northern entrance to the Kingsway Subway in Southampton Row, seen between 1906 and 1908, when the subway was only open as far as Aldwych station. *National Tramway Museum*

Above: To supplement the 16 Class F cars a further 34 were ordered in October 1905. Equipment and detail changes meant that they were classed as Class G and numbered 568-601. Here No 584 looks in pristine condition when photographed on 6 June 1907. *National Tramway Museum*

Below: Class F car No 556 working through the Kingsway section of the subway towards The Angel, Islington. Required to comply with regulations governing cars on tube railways, the trams were made from steel and other non-flammable materials, and each seated 36. As in railway tunnels, recesses were provided as refuges for workers or tram crews who had to walk through the subway. *National Tramway Museum*

Bridge. At this point the street had been constructed upon a viaduct built at the same time as the bridge, comprising 16 brick arches on brick piers, the tops of which were about 4ft below street level. As the subway had to go through some of these piers, they were examined and were found to have been sprung from timber frames which rested on old river mud from the former foreshore of the Thames. 'Considerable underpinning' of these piers was therefore required before work could begin on the subway itself.

Despite this, construction proceeded quickly, and after a special inspection of the completed works, the whole subway opened on 10 April 1908:

'... the first direct means of communication between the Council's tramway systems on the north and south of the Thames has been established. It is difficult to over-estimate the importance of this. ... [Previously, the tramway]

Above: Completion of the southern end of the Kingsway Subway, in 1907/8, required the creation of an arched entrance in the abutment of Waterloo Bridge. Seen early in 1908, the stonework looks finished, but the trackwork has a way to go yet.
National Tramway Museum

Below right: When completed, all but for a lick of paint on the new lamp standards, this is how the southern entrance to the Kingsway Subway looked when it opened on 10 April 1908. *IAL*

systems were separated from each other by long intervals, ... intercommunication between the various districts of London was considerably impeded, and ... a large central area unoccupied by tramways intervened between the respective termini, the lines breaking off abruptly in the middle of the street, all tramcars were obliged to discharge their passengers at dead-end terminals. Apart from the inconvenience to the travelling public, this caused a great congestion of traffic at the terminal points, diminishing the carrying power of the tramways by reason of the cross-shunting rendered necessary.'

Estimates put the cost of the second stage of the work at £145,000.

The Kingsway Subway was used by just two routes — 33 (West Norwood–Manor House) and 35 (Forest Hill–Highgate) — both worked by the Class F and G single-deckers. As these cars aged, and the inflexibility of having to work the subway with them grew ever more apparent,

the LCC formulated proposals to enlarge the subway for double-deck trams, so that more services could use it. A decision was taken to proceed with this in 1929, and the work was put out to tender. On 25 June 1929 the LCC considered seven tenders for the enlargement work. Against its own estimate of £210,810, the lowest tender was from Messrs John Cochrane & Sons, of 39 Victoria Street, London SW1, at £171,246 15s. This was accepted. Two weeks later the LCC also considered tenders for 150 new tramcars, 100 of which were of a new class — E/3 — to work the enlarged subway.

The first excavations on enlarging the Kingsway Subway were made on 9 September 1929. These involved placing 'a steel shield under the surface of Kingsway', the idea being that 'earth will then be removed above the present tunnel until the shield is reached, the shield thus forming the roof of the new tunnel'. This work also allowed the subway to remain open for the time being. Indeed, it was not

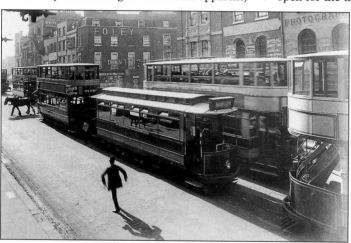

Left: Over the years, the restriction of using single-deck cars in the Kingsway Subway became a serious limitation on the planning and routing of tramway services, most of which were provided by double-deckers. Class F No 561 queues with 'E' and 'E/1' class cars whilst a horse and cart cross the road. Shadows reveal that the apparently one-legged man in the foreground is in fact a biped!
National Tramway Museum

Below left: A rare shot of the original Kingsway Subway in use. At 4.15pm on 23 March 1929, Class G car No 591, working route 35, waits at one of the subway's two stations. The photographer is under the watchful gaze of an Inspector.
Dr Hugh Nicol/Science Museum

Right: By December 1929, when Class G car No 600 was photographed, the original subway stock was showing its age. On 3 February 1930 the subway was closed for enlargement work and the 50 original Class F and G cars were withdrawn from service. *London Transport Museum*

Below right: Two views of the enlargement work carried out on the Kingsway Subway during 1930. The top one shows a new steel roof being installed in Southampton Row, whilst the bottom one shows the removal of the viaduct arches beneath Wellington Street, on the approach to Waterloo Bridge. *IAL*

necessary to close the subway for the enlargement work until 3 February 1930, when all the Class F and G cars were withdrawn from service. Work proceeded quickly, involving 500 workers, 24 hours a day; on 5 January 1931 it was announced that trial journeys were to begin that day for driver training, and that:

'The subway is now completed except for minor work at the two stations. During excavation 16,600 cubic yards of clay and ballast were removed, as was 1,135 tons of cast iron. New construction comprised 15,900 cubic yards of concrete and brickwork, 600 tons of new steelwork, and 135 tons of new cast iron. North of High Holborn the subway roof has been raised, two cast-iron tubes and brick arches (forming double tunnels) have been removed and a new steel roof on steel stanchions encased in concrete (forming one wide tunnel) has been substituted. ... Under the Strand ... the bottom halves of the two cast iron tubes have been removed and new concrete walls built to carry the top halves. The two tramway stations, Aldwych and Holborn, have been rebuilt and modernised. Both are brighter and larger. ... 5,000 journeys a week will be made through the subway.'

The enlarged subway was formally reopened on 14 January 1931. 'E/3' car No 1931, painted white and lined in blue, made the first journey. Public services resumed the following day, when a third route — 31 (Wandsworth (High Street)–Hackney Station) — was also introduced. The subway continued to prove its worth until it was closed as the focus of Stage 7 of Operation Tramaway on 5 April 1952. On 21 January 1964, a portion of the southern end of the subway reopened to road traffic as the Strand Underpass, but the northern portion, including the approach ramp and entrance in Southampton Row, and Holborn Station remain intact, abandoned and untroubled, save for the occasional visit from engineers and enthusiasts.

Above: An LCC Tramways poster advertising the reopened Kingsway Subway in 1931. *London Transport Museum*

Above right: 'E/3' class car No 1931, in a special livery of white lined with blue, emerges from the Kingsway Subway, having made a special journey through from Holborn as part of the reopening ceremony on 14 January 1931. *National Tramway Museum*

Right: Holborn station after enlargement, looking from the southbound platform to the northbound one. Notice how the station's name is at two levels, for passengers on each deck of the trams. *IAL*

Opposite above: On a (typically) wet July day in 1931, 'E/3' car No 1936 reaches street level in Southampton Row, having negotiated the Kingsway Subway en route to Highgate. *G. N. Southernden/ HCV Collection — L .B. Newham Library Service*

Opposite below: As part of the rebuilding of Waterloo Bridge, a new entrance to the subway was created, which involved alterations to the junction with the track along the Embankment. This shows the realignment work involved taking place in September 1937. *National Tramway Museum*

Above left: Ex-Leyton District Council 'E/3' No 191 is seen emerging into the sunlight from beneath the rebuilt Waterloo Bridge in the early 1950s. *V. C. Jones/IAL*

Above: The Kingsway Subway was popular for tours of the London tramways by enthusiasts' special cars, such as 'HR/2' class No 1885, seen running up to Southampton Row on 9 May 1948. Since tramway abandonment, these tracks are the only ones left uncovered in situ in central London. *V. C. Jones/IAL*

7. Current topics — The LCC's experiments with tramway operation

The LCC's decision to opt for the conduit system of current collection was thoroughly researched beforehand, notably by its Consultant Engineer, Prof Alexander Kennedy. It may therefore come as a surprise to learn that, in its first years of electric tramway operation, the Council undertook a number of experiments with other forms of current collection, traction, and service delivery.

The Streatham Hill cable tramway

One of the LCC's most bizarre experiments came within months of the inauguration of electric services on 15 May 1903. On 2 August 1903 it opened an extension to its lines in Kennington, which connected the electric tramway with the Streatham Hill cable tramway. Since the LCC's takeover of this cable line in 1899, it had been modified so that the cable gripper gear was a separate unit, capable of being attached beneath — and run out from under — ordinary horse trams, which could continue their journey into the city without the need for passengers to change cars. In order to offer the same through service to Streatham now that electricity had replaced horse traction, arrangements had been made to attach the cable gripper units to the four-wheeled Class B electric trams which were used on the route: 'Special cars are supplied in which the plough will be provided with a lifting apparatus so that it can be raised through an opening over the conduit at the place where the electric line ends and the cable line begins. The plough will lie close against the bottom of the car, while the gripper used on the cable-drawn cars will run into position.' This was a brilliant idea — on paper at least — but overlooked at least one important difference between horse and electric trams: their weight. A 56-seater electric tram could carry upwards of 2 tons more passengers than could a horse-car, and also had the additional weight of its motors and control equipment.

The inevitable happened: the cable could not take the additional load. By the end of September 1903, the local people had had enough: 'The patience of the inhabitants of Brixton and Streatham is becoming rapidly exhausted. The Kennington–Streatham cable line is proving very unreliable. It broke down for 90 minutes on Wednesday last [16 September] owing to a stoppage of the haulage cable. Troubles have been greatly increased since the adoption of the dual electric-cable system.' Nonetheless, the LCC persisted with the practice until the week beginning 19 October 1903:

'The unsuccessful attempt by the LCC to work their electric tramcars from Kennington-Streatham by means of the haulage cable has been abandoned. The Council have withdrawn all their electric cars from the Kennington-Streatham route. These cars have for some time been connected with the existing cable system at Kennington, and from there have continued the journey to Streatham village. It has been found, however, that the strain on the cable was too great. The cable cars have been reintroduced as far as Kennington, then passengers transfer to electric cars for the rest of the journey into the city. Only the old cable cars will henceforth be used until the route is electrified.'

With much embarrassment, arrangements were made to electrify the Streatham Hill tramway, and on 17 December 1903 the LCC Highways Committee recommended:

'the immediate reconstruction for electrical traction of the tramways between Kennington and Streatham, about seven miles of single lines. They claim that it is of great importance that this

Six photographs showing J. G. White & Co's workers reconstructing the Streatham Hill cable tramway for conduit operation, April–June 1904. Left: (top) jacking up the old rails; (middle) breaking up the old track with sledge-hammers and wedges; (bottom) setting in the conduit yokes and slot rail. Right: (top) putting in granite setts; (middle) bonding the conductor rails; (bottom) pitch-grouting. *IAL*

work should be completed with as little delay as possible, owing to the inconvenience which results from dealing with the traffic on these lines, which are now worked by cable traction, in conjunction with the lines which are worked by electric traction. An arrangement is now in force by which passengers on the Streatham lines who desire to travel to the various London termini have to change into the electrical cars at Kennington Gate, a course entailing grave inconvenience and discomfort, and, moreover, the receipts from the tramways are diminished owing to the absence of through car services. The conduit system is recommended, and it is proposed that the work should be put in hand

early in 1904. The cost is estimated at £90,000, exclusive of the outlay on rails, about £17,500. Electrical cars costing £47,686 have been ordered, and will soon be ready.'

On 22 December 1903 the full Council accepted this estimate of £90,000.

The conversion work was put out to tender, and on 2 March 1904 J. G. White & Co Ltd was awarded the contract for the conversion of the Streatham line to the conduit system:

'It was stipulated that the work must be finished by July 1st. When one considers the difficulty of tearing up 18,000ft of double cable line which has been well laid, and also allows for inevitable delays in the delivery of material, and the short notice given, it will be considered that the task of completion within the specified time was one calling for wide experience and first-class organisation. ... J. G. White & Co broke ground on April 6th. For the breaking up of the old cable road some interesting devices were adopted. ... In order to avoid the tedious process of unbolting the slot rail from the yokes, wedges of varying thickness were driven into the slot, whereby the rails were forced apart, carrying the shoulders of the yoke with them. ... During the first week the number of men employed was increased daily until some 1,600 were at work, and such progress had been made that on May 18th a car was run over the double line from Kennington Gate to Water Lane, a distance of 1¾ miles. ... The work was completed on June 13th, and the first car ran to the terminus on the 15th. The Board of Trade inspection was held on June 18th, and the line was thrown open for traffic on June 19th, seventeen days ahead of the stipulated date. There can be no doubt that, could the manufacturers have delivered material earlier, the whole work would have been completed by June 1st.'

On Sunday 19 June 1904, LCC electric tramcars ran for the first time between Blackfriars and Westminster bridges and Streatham. Conversion of the former cable line had taken just 44 days.

The 'G.B.' surface-contact trial — 1908/9

In his 1899 report, Prof Alexander Kennedy had looked favourably upon surface-contact systems of current collection, preferring them to conduit ones in that they were cheaper to install, not requiring such deep excavations. He also noted that there was then 'no large experience' of such systems in the country, but that, when this had been gained, the trial of a surface-contact system would be justified. Lincoln Tramways had operated the Griffiths-Bedell or 'G.B.' surface-contact system since 23 November 1905, and the firm that made it — G.B. Surface-Contact Co Ltd — was based in London. Early in 1908 the LCC decided to try the G.B. system for itself, and Dick, Kerr & Co converted the equivalent of 5.9 miles of single track in Mile End Road and Bow Road, between Bow and Aldgate:

'the current conductor is laid in vitrified stoneware pipes, which are then covered with concrete, the total depth excavated not exceeding 19in. The insulators are of vitrified and glazed clay, and are furnished with an

Dick, Kerr & Co's workers converting track in Mile End and Bow roads to the Griffiths-Bedell surface-contact system. A series of trials, in the early hours of six days in March 1909, failed to convince the LCC of the merits of surface-contact systems, and this equipment was removed within four months of the trials' ending. *IAL*

earthing device, which is connected at intervals to the rails. The studs have cast-iron heads, which are flush with the rest of the paving, and they are embedded in blocks of granite, which stand the traffic the same as the rest of the setts. Current is collected by the car from the studs by means of a chain of iron links spring-suspended within one pole of the magnet, the bottom face of which moves over the stud-head. The collection of current is then purely magnetic, and it is claimed that not only is leakage totally prevented, but that it is difficult for a stud to be left alive. The roadway is quite unobstructed, as the studs do not project above the level of the surrounding surface.'

On 21 June 1908 the Board of Trade inspected the G.B. system, and the following day gave it a six-month certificate, permitting trial runs to begin. These were conducted by W. M. Mordey of the G.B. Surface-Contact Co. The full six months was, however, not required, and the original installation proved unsatisfactory. On 1 October 1908 Mr Mordey reported on a series of improvements that were required, and, once these had been made, the trials resumed, under a new certificate. This is a record of trials conducted in early mornings during March 1909:

5 March	1.30 to 3.30am — icy — ran equivalent of eight miles
6 March	1.30 to 3.15am — cold — also ran eight miles New device (to prevent arcing) working well
9 March	trial runs with Mr Trotter, Board of Trade
10 March	more trial runs
23 March	12.40 to 3.40am — road wet and muddy.

During this period the system suffered from a number of permanently-live studs, one of which electrocuted a horse, but, as Mr Mordey put it, the 'good point is that, although the stud was fully alive and all the conditions very favourable to severe shock, the horse was not killed. … [Its owners] have reported … that it is satisfactorily recovering and should be at work again in a few days.' Quite the optimist, he also dismissed the

breakage of the chain collector on several occasions, and noted that his last run on 23 March had been 'admirable and sparkless'. Overall, in a report written on 31 March 1909, Mr Mordey felt that 'comparatively little preliminary running is likely to be necessary to get the whole line into satisfactory order'. The LCC did not agree. It cancelled the trials, converting the track to work partly on the conduit and partly on overhead wires, and reopened it as such on 31 July 1909.

The LCC Tramways and overhead wires — 1908

LCC Tramways' first experience of overhead wires had come in 1908, when it opened extensions of conduit lines that joined up with tramways operated by Bexley UDC and the LUT, both of which used the overhead system. First to open was Beresford Square, Woolwich–Plumstead Church on 17 April 1908, followed by Harrow Road, Harlesden–Hammersmith on 30 May 1908, extended to Putney on 23 January 1909. To permit through-running from the conduit to the overhead sections, both the cars and track had to be altered. The ploughs and their carriers had to be altered so that the former could be slid out from either side; the track had to be modified so that overhead and conduit overlapped for a short section, and that within this distance the conduit slot moved from the centre of the rails to outside them, allowing for the removal or insertion of a plough. Thus was born another distinctive feature of the LCC Tramways — the change-pit.

An overhead line opened in 1910 called for still more innovation. It ran between Woolwich and Eltham Church via Well Hall Road, but fell foul of an agreement with the Royal Observatory at Greenwich that any tramway built within a three-mile radius of the Observatory should use an insulated electrical system for fear that its delicate instruments would be affected by the earth-return currents on the line. To overcome this, a twin-wire overhead was used which offered an insulated current-return circuit away from the ground. The Woolwich–Eltham Church line opened on 23 July 1910. Its working required cars to be equipped with twin trolley-poles, plus additional

'M' class car No 1433 was one of 10 fitted with a pair of trolley poles to work the twin-wire overhead route — Woolwich–Eltham Church — which opened on 23 July 1910. The unusual approach was to avoid disturbing sensitive instruments in the Royal Observatory, Greenwich, with earth returns.
National Tramway Museum

On 29 November 1920 the twin-wire system was used on a new section of tramway from Lee Green to Eltham (Lyme Farm), and on 22 March 1921 the opening of a twin-wire section between Eltham (Lyme Farm) and Eltham Church joined these to the rest of the Woolwich tramways. 'E/1' class cars Nos 1360-1400 were fitted with twin trolley poles to work the Eltham lines. 'E/1' No 1399 is seen in March 1927 — near the end of twin-wire operation, as the Royal Observatory moved to Scotland later that year. *Dr Hugh Nicol/Science Museum*

switching to allow them to operate over the conduit, and overhead using one and two wires, although the Woolwich tramways were not linked to the conduit until 5 April 1914. To work the twin-wire service, 10 'M' class four-wheeled cars, Nos 1428-1437, and four 'E/1' class cars, Nos 1350-1353, were fitted with twin trolley-poles. On 29 November 1920 the twin-wire system was also used on a new section of tramway from Lee Green to Eltham (Lyme Farm), and on 22 March 1921 the opening of another new section of twin-wire tramway between Eltham (Lyme Farm) and Eltham Church joined these sections to the rest of the Woolwich tramways. 'E/1' class cars

Nos 1360-1400 were fitted with twin trolley-poles to work the Eltham lines. The system remained in use until the Royal Observatory at Greenwich removed to Scotland in 1927.

The LCC's trailer cars — 1911–24

LCC Tramways also became interested in the operation of trailer cars, and on 7 November 1905 the Council resolved to ask the Board of Trade to amend its bylaws so that trailer cars could be run. The Board agreed that they could, but only for the 'conveyance of stores and sand to and from tramway depots, between the hours of 10pm and 6am'. In 1909, the use of trailer cars became a very 'hot issue' amongst tramway operators, and the LCC applied again to the Board of Trade. On 8 January 1910 the latter agreed to the use of trailer cars on the route from Euston Road to Hampstead Heath, but the cars were not to be run between 10am and 5pm, which effectively ruled out passenger use. One year later the LCC had another go. To gain experience of trailer-car use it modified a pair of 'G'-class cars — Nos 572 and 573 — to work coupled together. This 'unit' was inspected by

Above: Regular trailer-car services from Clapham began on 23 July 1913, using eight converted ex-North Metropolitan Tramways horse trams withdrawn from trailer trials in Woolwich the previous month. Here one of the cars is drawn out of Clapham depot to work route 2 to Merton. *London Transport Museum*

Right: Based on its experience with the eight converted horse trams, the LCC ordered 150 purpose-built trailer cars — Nos T9-T158. The first of the class, No T9, is seen in a newly-completed turning loop near Nightingale Lane, Clapham, in January 1915.
National Tramway Museum

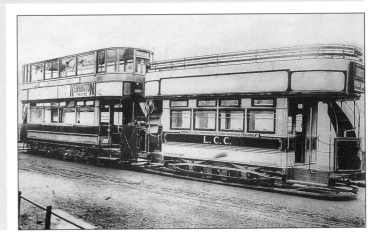

A well-patronised 'E' class car with trailer T24 on Victoria Embankment in early August 1915, shortly after the cars were introduced on the Merton route. Trailer cars were phased out between 1922 and 17 April 1924, when the last one ran in service. *National Tramway Museum*

the Board of Trade on 13 January 1911 and sanctioned for trial use on the above line. This began on 17 January, the coupled cars running between 7.00am and 9.00am and after 7.00pm, but was abruptly cancelled when action was taken by the Metropolitan Police on 1 February 1911 following a derailment. The trials resumed between 15 April and 13 May, and again on 5 July, but the Police's concern mounted, and on 14 August 1911 Aubrey Fell, General Manager of LCC Tramways, received a letter from Commissioner of Police of the Metropolis, who felt that 'no advantages are likely to accrue which would in any way compensate for the obstruction and dangers incidental to the use of trailer cars.' He hoped that 'the Council may be able to employ some other method of attaining the end they have in view which will not be so harmful to the interest of all other traffic.'

Unwilling to let the matter rest there, the LCC included trailer operation in its (Tramways & Improvements) Bill 1912, where it formed Clause 26. Evidence covering this was considered by a House of Commons Committee on 10-11 July 1912. Among those giving evidence was Aubrey Fell:

Q: 'You have considered various means of tackling the problem [of people that come at rush hours]?'
Fell: 'Yes.'
Q: 'Have you come to the conclusion that the only way to tackle that problem in London is to run cars coupled together?'
Fell: 'Yes.'
Q: 'If you run two tramway cars coupled together you have one unit of traffic?'
Fell: 'Yes.'

Q: 'Is the advantage … that you have double the seating capacity for a unit of traffic than you have in the case of a single car?'

Fell: 'Yes.'

Q: 'Two cars coupled together will deal more effectively with a large crowd than two single cars running one after another at a short interval?'

Fell: 'Yes, very much more effectively.'

Q: 'The trailer car will have three entrances?'

Fell: 'Yes. There will be no brakesman or motorman on the second car; therefore that platform can be utilised for taking passengers on and off.'

Q: 'Is the running of trailer cars beneficial to the general traffic in the street?'

Fell: 'It would pick up the passengers more quickly, and at a cross road the two cars coupled together would get much more quickly across at the junction than two separate cars.'

Eventually the Committee agreed to the use of trailer cars by the LCC, but retained the right to sanction the routes and the time of running of the trailers.

The LCC commenced trailer-car operation on its Eltham routes on 20 March 1913, using converted horse-tram bodies. Eight such cars — numbered T1-T8 — were used initially. Deemed a success, trailer-car use was widened and 150 purpose-built trailer cars ordered. These were numbered T9-T158 and were used on a number of routes between 1914 and the end of trailer-car operation by the LCC on 17 April 1924.

The LCC's petrol-electric tramcars — 1913

At the same time as it introduced trailer-car operation, the LCC also experimented with three petrol-electric tramcars. Essentially electric tramcars that generated their own electricity, these were also based around old horse-tram bodies fitted to specially-made trucks. A 40hp petrol engine was housed under the stairs on one platform, and was coupled to a generator which produced 350V. The engine and motors, plus all of the control equipment, was made by W. A. Stevens Ltd at Maidstone. The cars, numbered P1-P3, were designed for use on a former horse tramway which ran

One of three petrol-electric tramcars introduced in 1913 on a former horse tramway which ran through areas whose local authorities refused the use of conventional electric traction. They were numbered P1-P3 and entered service on 10 July 1913. *IAL*

In petrol-electric cars P1-P3, a 40hp petrol engine was housed under the stairs on one platform, as seen here. Unfortunately, this proved noisy and costly, and gave off choking petrol fumes, which resulted in their withdrawal on 9 December 1913, after only five months' service. *IAL*

In its final months the LCC conducted experiments with both bow collectors and pantographs in place of trolley poles. These used a section of line to Grove Park, opened on 15 November 1928, on which the overhead was modified for use by the collectors. 'E/1s' 835 and 1360 were fitted with bow collectors; the former is seen at Grove Park terminus. *National Tramway Museum*

'E/1' cars Nos 844 and 1172 were used to test pantographs, the latter being seen in the same location at Grove Park. The tests were inconclusive. Use of the collectors required alterations to the cars and overhead, but a major shake-up in London's tramway history was on the horizon, so they were not pursued. *National Tramway Museum*

through Bethnal Green, Hackney and Stepney, whose local authorities forbade the use of conventional electric traction. Unfortunately,

this kind proved noisy and costly, and gave off choking petrol fumes; they ran in service only from 10 July to 9 December 1913.

8. 'Current is cheap compared with lost passengers' — The innovative work of Christopher Spencer and the Underground Group

No one did more to further the design and performance of London's trams than Christopher Spencer, Tramways Manager of the Underground Group of companies. In the autumn of 1919 he was part of a deputation of four senior Group managers who visited cities on the East Coast of the USA to study their transport systems, and returned with his head full of ideas. Spencer had been particularly impressed with the use of single-decker cars, coupled together at peak times, but also operated singly by just the driver. He was also taken with American ideas on passenger flow through these cars by the use of separate entrance and exit doors. Combining these with powerful motors and air or hydraulic brakes made for modern, efficient and flexible public transport.

On Easter Monday 1920, single-deck MET Type E car No 132 was damaged in a runaway accident with a steam wagon near Alexandra Palace. Withdrawn from service, the car was put into store, but later in the year, using the insurance payment from the accident, it was rebuilt as the first practical embodiment of Christopher Spencer's ideas. When it emerged, the car had been shortened to 21ft, and the platforms had been enlarged so that passengers could enter and leave by whichever was the front end. Tickets were issued by the driver, using an automatic machine, and he had powerful hydraulic track brakes at hand. The car performed well and offered savings in operating costs, so further experiments were sanctioned, although No 132 was sold on to the LUT in 1922, and extensively rebuilt.

The LUT's experience with No 132 was so favourable that Spencer rebuilt three more cars, Nos 175, 178 and 275, which reappeared in 1924 as Nos 342-344. They were met with acclaim by the trade press, which examined No 342 in November 1924:

After passing to the LUT, experimental MET rebuild No 132 re-emerged as LUT No 341, restored to its original length. It was tried on route 77 (Richmond Park Gates–Tolworth) in 1923, and moved to route 55 (Hanwell–Brentford) in 1924. It is seen here at Fulwell depot in 1923. The car was the first fully-vestibuled one to run in London. *IAL*

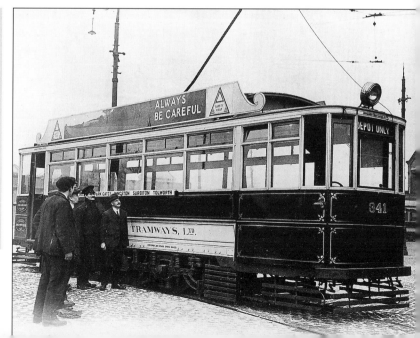

Left: LUT car No 342 was a rebuild of No 175, embodying many of Christopher Spencer's American ideas. It was introduced in November 1924. Front-entrance/rear-exit, the car made extensive use of compressed air for braking and operating the interlocked doors and steps. Seating 30, the 'one-man car' enabled a 10min service to be run at less cost than a 15min one using 'two-man' double-deckers. *Real Photographs/IAL*

Below left: The driver's platform of LUT No 342, showing the layout of the controls. Missing from this view are the foot-operated farebox and a change machine, which were mounted on the curved frame behind the seat. Further to emphasise the importance of standing on the pressure-plate for the exit door to open, it was clearly coloured red. *London Transport Museum*

'It had been found that single trucks were not as comfortable as bogie trucks, and a new vehicle has been built on bogie trucks which embodies the results of the experience gained during the past two years. ... With the adoption of the bogie trucks it was found necessary to adopt air brakes ... giving the advantage that the same compressor is available for the automatic control of the doors. The door arrangements are very ingenious. Both entrance and exit doors are on the off-side, and the driver has control of them separately. They are automatically prevented from opening whilst the car is in motion, irrespective of whether the car is travelling on power or brake, or coasting in the "off" position. This is arranged by means of a specially designed solenoid-operated valve, which shuts off the air supply for opening the doors, except when the car is practically stationary. ... The entrance door will then open, but the exit door will not unless a passenger is waiting on the rear platform, because this door is fitted with a valve which is controlled by a tread-plate in the rear platform, on which a person must be standing to open the door. ... The doors and steps work in unison, the steps being folded when the doors are shut and vice versa. ... Air brakes are fitted which act both on the wheels and on the track. ... The air brake is fitted with a "dead-man" grip. ... Passengers drop their coin into a fare box which is foot-operated by the driver ... [who] is provided with a seat, and ... large windscreen wipers to ensure clear vision in wet weather.'

A rare insight into Christopher Spencer's thoughts regarding the 'Modernising of Tramcars' is given under this title in an article he contributed to *The Electric Railway And Tramway Journal* of 17 July 1925: 'Under the deluge of criticism levelled against tramcars, the public have almost lost sight of the fact that the modern tramcar ... is a very different vehicle to its pre-war brother. This is not surprising, because there has been generally no noticeable alteration made as regards external appearance, and although the equipment has been vastly improved, the only visible difference internally has been the use of white paint.' Spencer had fitted new lightweight motors to 40 cars, and found improved acceleration from a standing start:

Speed (mph)	New equipment (sec)	Old equipment (sec)
12	8	9
14	10	13
16	13	19
20	24	52

Paramount for Spencer were passenger comfort and standards, and his remarks on this topic are as interesting for what they imply about other London tramcars as for what they say about his improved ones:

'The standard of comfort of travelling in London has made such strides during recent years that this factor has become a very important one where competitive forms of transport are provided. It must be admitted that from this aspect tramcars generally have not made any real advance since they first appeared twenty years ago ... with hardwood seats, and no real pretensions to comfort. The internal appearance of the cars has received careful consideration, and several cars have been entirely re-decorated in harmonising colour schemes, such as light oak and white enamel, white and French grey, cream and brown, etc. The main experiment with seating has been with cross seats. Apparently, the London public has taken kindly to [these] for instead of looking at their opposite passenger they can look out of the window in the direction of travel. The designing of really comfortable cross seats for tramcars is complicated by the necessity for reversing the back at the termini. This difficulty has been got over ... by mechanically connecting the seat to the back so that the former moves forward slightly, and also tilts so that the maximum comfort is obtained in either direction. For the first time in London transport the top deck has also been fitted with spring upholstered seats and backs, both deck[s'] seats being covered with moquette of pleasing blue and fawn colouring. ... Amongst the other details are open handgrips of washable material on hand straps. ... This type of car will certainly give luxury to travelling. The seating capacity is reduced by a total of six seats, but the tramcar, if it is to evolve out of its chrysalis state of being chiefly the workman's vehicle, must follow the lead of the omnibus and give the public comfort and attractiveness. The day has passed when utilitarianism is the only thing that matters, and the tramcar can do all the omnibus does, both in comfort and utility, and more. The London public demand comfort to-day, vide the pit at the best theatres, Lyon's teashops, etc., but the average fare is only about 1½d or about ten minutes riding, and the thought in the past has been that, for such short distance travel, comfort was of secondary importance. ... Quick acceleration and deceleration, with good average speed, luxury, and safety are the present-day requirements of the London public, and so to supply this costs money in current and other directions, but current is cheap compared with lost passengers.'

The Underground Group introduced many of Christopher Spencer's improvements during 1926, and early the following year this enabled it to claim that the new rolling stock was 'proving

A close-up of one of Christopher Spencer's 'really comfortable cross seats'. By mechanically connecting the seat to the back, the former moved forward slightly, and also tilted to give maximum comfort in either direction. *Modern Transport/IAL*

exceedingly popular, and evidenced by the hundreds of appreciative letters received by the management', and also to claim both an average speed 'higher than that on any other system in the country' and a fall in the number of delays due to mechanical and electrical defects 'from 11.0 to 2.9 per 10,000 miles run, good testimony to the methods employed'.

Spencer's experiments were also extended to double-deck cars in 1926, with the construction of two experimental trams. Pooling the expertise within the Underground Group of companies, engineers at the London General Omnibus Co (LGOC) were consulted over the body design for the cars. In 1923 the LGOC had introduced its 'NS'-type motorbus, which featured a lightweight body design that had gone on to prove highly successful. Two tramcars were planned, one to be built by the MET at Hendon, the other to be designed and built around 'NS'-type bus components by the LGOC. Both vehicles were launched to the press on 3 March 1927.

The MET designed and built car No 318, which was nicknamed 'Bluebell' because 'it had been painted on the outside in a pleasing shade of light blue'. Making the body from steel-clad ash channels clad in aluminium panels saved almost 4 tons over conventional methods, and produced a tramcar with an unloaded weight of just over 12 tons that seated 71 passengers. Allied to powerful lightweight motors, which alone saved over 1,000lb in weight, this produced a car capable of high performance, reaching 25mph from a standing start in 150yd. No 318 included all of the innovations introduced by Spencer on single-deckers Nos 342-344 with regards to passenger flow, only reversed, with rear entrance/front exit, combined with the same door-interlocking and braking arrangements. Its interior had been designed to be 'as free as possible from all mouldings or corners which would be liable to collect dirt, and the colouring has been selected to give a harmonious and bright appearance with due regard to serviceability, the lower panel being coloured French grey with white enamelled ceilings. Stainless steel is used for all band railing and hand grip stanchions. In the top saloon, each window is constructed to open by

MET-designed and -built No 318 was launched to the press on 3 March 1927. The lightweight body saved almost 4 tons over conventional designs. Although the vestibules were enclosed, the front panel was left unglazed to comply with local regulations. The Palmolive advert was painted on: when the soap firm's painters turned up at Hendon to apply this, the MET's painters threatened to strike over the issue. *Modern Transport/IAL*

vertical slide, and is of the balanced type operable individually by passengers.'

The LGOC designed and built a car that was supposed to be No 319, but which, by mistake, was numbered 139. Essentially two 'NS'-type bus bodies back to back, it was painted in that company's characteristic red colour, from which its corresponding nickname 'Poppy' was derived. The most striking characteristic of the lightweight body, which was similar in construction to that on 'Bluebell', was the prominent driver's cabs, which stood proud of the main body, a feature that would be seen again. Passengers entered and exited the car from the rear platform, and the seats in both saloons rotated around a central pivot, enabling the use of fixed backs 'designed with a special spring so arranged that the centre portion is more easily compressed than the outside edge which makes for comfort and prevents any discomfort due to sway when passing round curves'.

LGOC-designed and -built MET No 139 'Poppy' was intended to be No 319! Essentially two 'NS'-type bus bodies back to back, passengers boarded and exited from the rear platform only. The prominent but unglazed driver's cabs were a departure that would be seen again.
National Tramway Museum

Left: 'Poppy' was transferred to the LUT on 16 November 1927, in whose fleet she became No 350, seen here in the autumn of 1928. *Dr Hugh Nicol/ Science Museum*

Below left: MET No 320 was nicknamed 'Blossom'. The original bogies proved too lightweight and were replaced with ones of a heavier design. On re-entering service the car worked route 40 from Finchley. On 4 August 1929 she was photographed at Golders Green terminus with a well-regimented inspector standing to attention alongside. *G. N. Southernden/ HCV Collection — L.B. Newham Library Service*

Right: Inside the driver's cab of MET No 320. The driver sat on a stool to allow those drivers unaccustomed to sitting down to drive from a standing position. A roof-light was also let into the cab to illuminate the controls directly. *Modern Transport/IAL*

Part of the 'Bluebell'/'Poppy' experiment was to canvass the opinions of the people who used the cars: 'The public who use these services have been encouraged to contribute suggestions, and many thousands of passengers have acceded to the company's request and, in some cases, have contributed ideas which have been of great value.' The use of 'some' in relation to 'many thousands' speaks for itself, but this information, combined with experience gained from operating the two cars, was used to design and build a further three experimental tramcars for the MET, which appeared between April 1929 and June 1930. They were designed by W. S. Graf-Baker, Assistant Engineer to the Underground Group's railways, and built by the Union Construction & Finance Co Ltd (UCC) in its works at Feltham, Middlesex. The first to appear was MET No 320 in April 1929. This incorporated the passenger-flow principles from the single-deckers, with the large platforms from 'Bluebell', and the prominent forward cab from 'Poppy'. The body was an all-steel lattice

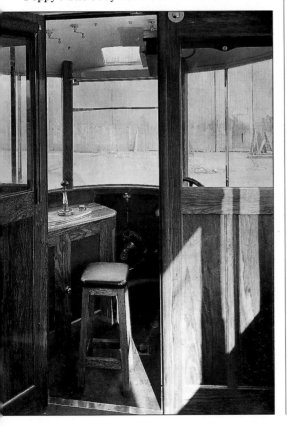

construction, with aluminium panels for all but the dashes. At just under 41ft in length, the car was the longest yet seen on any London tramway. Added to this was the adoption of equal wheel bogies, with each axle powered by a 35hp motor. Praise was heaped upon the new 64-seater tram: 'It provides everything which modern conditions demand, rapid acceleration, high speed, the maximum of passenger comfort, ample lighting, and so far as human ingenuity can devise, the elimination of superfluous noise.'

The second experimental car, MET No 330, was completed in October 1929. It was six inches shorter than No 320, but overall it closely resembled the earlier car, save for a more rounded and tapered end styling, and the body panels were all aluminium this time. Planned as a second four-motor car, last-minute problems over suitable control equipment saw the substitution of single-motor maximum-traction bogies, each with one 60hp motor. Again based on the rear entrance/front exit principle, the major innovation on No 330 was the adoption of a 'Pay As You Enter' fare-collection system. To assist this, the staircases rose up from the rear of the platforms, rather than from off the front of them as on No 320, in an attempt to prevent jams: 'The conductor is seated in the rear vestibule before a special ticket-issuing machine and collects fares as passengers board the car. The conductor remaining seated, he can more satisfactorily control the movements of the car and signals to the driver, thereby affecting a speeding up in actual operation. Passengers also will no longer be disturbed by the conductor moving about the car during the journey.' MET No 330 entered service on 6 November 1929.

The third and final experimental tramcar built by UCC was MET No 331, which entered service in June 1930. This represented a more radical departure from all of the passenger-flow experiments conducted to date, in that it had a centre-entrance and -exit arrangement, commonly seen on European tramways. It had been intended that the conductor would issue tickets from a machine mounted on a column in the centre of the entrance vestibule, but this arrangement was removed between the press launch of the car and its entering service later in the year, because tests had shown that it caused congestion.

Above: MET Nos 320 and 330 pass whilst working route 40 (North Finchley–Cricklewood). The end-styling differences between the two cars are emphasised, with 330's more rounded and tapered form highlighted.
London Transport Museum

Left: A three-quarter view of MET No 330 taken on her press launch early in November 1929.
Modern Transport/IAL

Above left: Detail of the rear entrance of MET No 330 showing the air-operated doors and steps, the angle and position of the stairs. *Modern Transport/IAL*

Above: A view of No 2 end on MET No 330, showing the seven-step stairs, platform and the 'Pay As You Pass' conductor's position on the right-hand side. *Modern Transport/IAL*

Left: The front exit of MET No 330. Each platform had a 30sq ft capacity. *Modern Transport/IAL*

Below: Seating on the top deck of MET No 330 was covered in a blue-grey pantasote, and was across the car save for two four-person side seats at each end. *Modern Transport/IAL*

The final experimental MET car, No 331, at a press launch in June 1930. Apart from the central entrance/exit, the driving cabs were also higher than on MET Nos 320 and 330 owing to the use of full-height controllers. The car ran on the bogies originally intended for No 330 and was reputedly nicknamed 'Cissie'.
Modern Transport/IAL

With eight years' experimentation and experience, Christopher Spencer and the Underground Group were well placed to finalise a design for a large order for 100 new tramcars which had been agreed. These were to be split, with the LUT taking 46 and the MET taking 54, plus No 331. The final design was again in the hands of W. S. Graf-Baker. All of the best features of the previous experimental cars were incorporated. The cars were of the rear-entrance/front-exit pattern, with platform vestibules and stairs arranged as on No 320. They rode on maximum-traction bogies, like No 330, but shared No 331's higher cabs, which some thought less pleasing than the ones on the earlier car. The cars were again constructed by UCC at Feltham — the name that would quickly be adopted for them. The LUT got its 'Felthams' into service first, introducing them on its Shepherds Bush–Uxbridge route on 5 January 1931, the MET cars first working the Cricklewood–Finchley route on 1 February 1931.

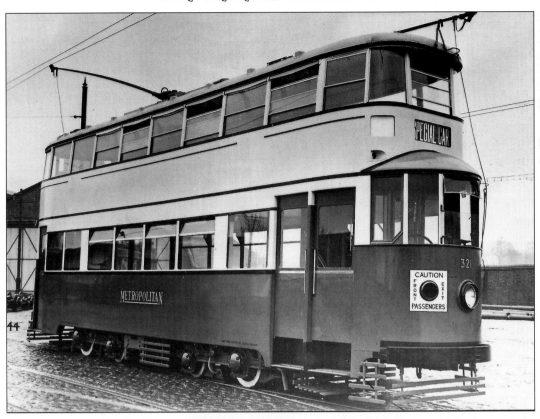

Above: MET 'Feltham' No 321 photographed at Finchley depot in January 1931. The cars were conduit-fitted for through-running over LCC tracks. Some people felt the high driver's cabs, carried over from No 331, spoiled the line of the cars, compared to No 330. *Modern Transport/IAL*

Right: One of the platforms and driving cabs on MET No 321, showing the driver's seat which was integral with the door. Once this was closed, and the driver seated, a bolt engaged, preventing the door from being opened. *Modern Transport/IAL*

Left: A close-up of the electrical control equipment on MET No 321. To the right are the line contactors — one to each trolley pole — and the circuitry interlocking the door mechanisms with the controllers to prevent the car from moving off with the doors open. *Modern Transport/IAL*

Below left: In the lower saloon, MET 'Feltham' No 321 had 22 seats covered in a green lozenge-pattern moquette. Each car was also licensed to carry 10 standee passengers on each end platform. *Modern Transport/IAL*

Right: In the upper saloon, MET 'Feltham' No 321 had 42 seats, covered in grained red Rexine. Lest the drop-down windows encouraged it, each was adorned with a 'DO NOT LEAN OUT OF THE WINDOW' notice. *Modern Transport/IAL*

Below right: To keep its new 'Feltham' fleet pristine, the MET invested in a high-pressure-water washing system, seen here in use on No 359 at Finchley depot. The nozzles are by the cleaners' hands, activated by a grip lever in the other hand. *Modern Transport/IAL*

Far right: The insides of the 'Felthams' were kept clean by using Sturtevant Turbine Suction Cleaners, a pair of which can be seen in use in Finchley depot. Two kinds of nozzle were available — one for the floor (left) and one for the cushions (right). Will the chap on the right tell his mate that he's missed that 1d ticket, though? *Modern Transport/IAL*

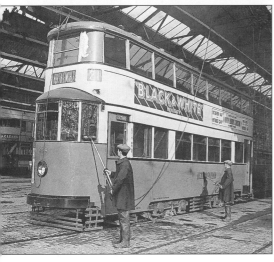

9. 'Pullmanisation' — The modernisation of the LCC tramcars

Joshua Bruce succeeded Aubrey Fell as General Manager of the LCC Tramways in 1924. He had worked for the undertaking since 20 October 1903, when he became Traffic Manager, rising to Deputy Chief Officer by 1910. On taking up his new post in 1924, Bruce would have been aware of the improvements being made to the tramcars operated by the LUT and MET, and to the strides being taken in motorbus design by the LGOC. By comparison, the LCC's tramway fleet looked and felt old-fashioned. During his six-year tenure as General Manager, Joshua Bruce would change this.

Through the trade press, and the general 'grapevine' that exists within any industry, Bruce would have learned in detail what Christopher Spencer was doing to modernise the LUT and MET cars; he would also have been all too aware of the difference between working in the 'private sector', as Spencer did, and in the 'public' one, as he did. In the mid-1920s, perhaps the starkest contrast between tram and bus travel was in the level of comfort provided. The newer buses, such as the LGOC's 'NS' type, had upholstered seats and bright interiors, whilst the LCC's trams retained their bent and slatted wood seats and 'gloomy' natural-wood interiors.

Through discussion, a progressive programme of tramcar improvement was devised. Improved cars would receive:

- upholstered cross seats — two and one — in the lower deck
- upholstered seat cushions, retaining wooden backs, on the upper deck
- interiors on both decks painted white, with improved lighting
- a new red and cream livery, and
- body- rather than truck-mounted plough carriers.

Trams so treated would be described as 'Pullman' cars, and the process of improving them thus was termed 'Pullmanisation'. The first car to receive this treatment was 'E/1' class No 1817, which returned to service on 24 June 1926; the second car to be Pullmanised was 'E/1' class No 1675. Public reaction was favourable, and it was decided to assess the tramcar fleet for its suitability for the same treatment. Out of around 1,800 cars, only 200 were deemed unsuitable to receive the improvements. These were mainly older cars, notably Classes C and M, which were used on the hilly routes up Dog Kennel Hill, Dulwich, and Highgate Hill. Accordingly, between 1926 and March 1930, 1,450 LCC tramcars were Pullmanised, including all of the 'E' and 'E/1' class cars.

On 10 July 1928 the LCC Highways Committee reported on the need to replace 150 older tramcars that were unsuitable for Pullmanisation. Taking account of the planned enlargement of the Kingsway Subway, at least 50 double-deckers would be needed to replace the Class F and G single-deck subway cars, and about the same number would be needed to replace the Class C and M hilly-route cars. The use of common components for all the cars, despite their different applications, also made sense, as did ordering them as one batch. Hardest to plan were the hilly-route trams, and in the autumn of 1928 it was decided to build two prototype cars which would be run in service for evaluatory purposes. Constructed at Charlton Works, the cars had equal wheel bogies, with each axle powered by a separate motor, but differed with regard to their bodies. The first, classified 'HR/1' — for 'hilly route' — used a spare prototype body, identical to those intended for the latest batch of 'E/1s', which were to use equipment from the soon-to-be-withdrawn 'F' and 'G' class subway cars. The car became No 1852. The second used an all-metal body, itself an experiment for the 150 cars soon to be ordered. It was classified 'HR/2' and became No 1853. Internally, both cars had the by now standard 'Pullman' finish.

Both cars were placed in service on Dog Kennel Hill on 26 April 1929, after one of them had been inspected by the Ministry of Transport, which requested a report on their general working after they had been in operation for six months. When this was produced, the cars were found to have been 'entirely successful; they have not given trouble in operation; and they are popular with the platform staff as well as with the public on

account of their excellent riding qualities and general comfort'. Of the two, No 1853 was preferred, because its body gave 5in extra internal width on the top deck, due to its new structural framework. The general-use tramcars were to have maximum-traction bogies, and to be classified 'E/3'. On 23 July 1929, the LCC approved an estimate of £453,000 for 150 new trams (100 Class E/3, and 50 Class HR/2), plus an estimate of £182,500 for a further 60 'HR/2s'.

Before any of these new cars was delivered, in early March 1930 the LCC put into service an 'E/1' car (No 1506) which had an experimental glazed-vestibule front fitted. The use of special

Right: The crew of 'E/3' car No 1946 model the standard Pullman 'two and one' seating on the lower deck, plus the better look created by a white interior and improved lighting.
V. C. Jones/IAL

Below: No 112 was one of the second order of 'HR/2s', which were delivered in 1931. They came with their vestibule fronts already fitted, but none carried trolley poles as they were confined exclusively to conduit routes only. The car is seen at Dog Kennel Hill in July 1932.
G. N. Southernden/HCV Collection — L .B. Newham Library Service

Above: 'HR/2' No 155 is seen c1934 sporting the LPTB's new standard livery. The equal-wheel bogies can also be seen to good effect. *IAL*

Left: Unlike older wooden-framed cars, the 'HR/2' bodies retained their lines until the end of their days in service. No 1877 is seen here on a tour organised by the Southern Counties Touring Society, which arranged many trips around the remaining South London tramways in their final years. *IAL*

non-splinterable glass had convinced the Metropolitan Police to sanction the trial. Different windscreens were fitted to either end, with one or two opening louvres, and with or without a wiper. At the end of the trial the two-louvre, no-wiper style of windscreen was judged to be the best, and in August 1931 it was decided to fit similar screens to all suitable cars. The frames were made from 'Alpax' lightweight aluminium alloy, and were in three parts, allowing partial replacement in the case of damage. First to receive the new vestibules were the 100 new 'E/3' cars.

In the first week of June 1930, the first of the new fleet of Pullman tramcars was put into service, a fitting achievement for Joshua Bruce, who retired as General Manager that month; he was succeeded by Theodore Thomas. The bulk of the new trams entered service during July 1930. Beforehand, the press had the opportunity to inspect examples at Charlton Works:

'Seating on both decks is roomy and comfortable. In the lower saloon the upholstering is of the Council's standard pattern moquette, while for the upper deck seats and seat backs a special type of non-inflammable red leather cloth is used. The padding and covering of the seat backs in addition to the main seats on the upper deck is a recent innovation which is much

Right: In early March 1930 the LCC put 'E/1' No 1506 into service fitted with an experimental glazed vestibule front. Different windscreens were fitted to either end, with one or two opening louvres, and with or without a wiper.
National Tramway Museum

Below right: The first of the new fleet of 'E/3' tramcars was put into service in the first week of June 1930, and the bulk of them had entered service by that July, which is when this example was photographed. Like the 'HR/2' seen on page 3, this does not 'hide its light'.
London Transport Museum

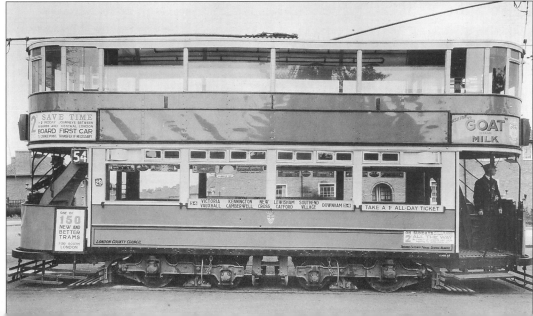

"English Electric"

Builders of L.C.C. Tramcars.

The illustrations show one of 50 Modern Tramcars built by The English Electric Company for the L.C.C. Tramways. The small pictures show the comfortable seating arrangements in the lower and upper saloons. A further **50 Double-Deck all-steel Tramcars** and **100 equipments** are now under construction at our Preston Works.

ENGLISH ELECTRIC
THE ENGLISH ELECTRIC COMPANY LIMITED.
HEAD OFFICE:
Queen's House, Kingsway, London,W.C.2.

Works: BRADFORD, COVENTRY, PRESTON, RUGBY, STAFFORD.

BRANCH OFFICES AND ASSOCIATES ABROAD:
ARGENTINE, AUSTRALIA, BRAZIL, CANADA, COLOMBO, EGYPT, FRANCE, INDIA, JAPAN, NEW ZEALAND, SOUTH AFRICA, STRAITS SETTLEMENTS AND F.M.S.

Above: The bodies for 50 'E/3' cars (Nos 161-210) were built by English Electric, which proudly advertised this fact in the trade press. The cars were actually purchased by Leyton District Council, but numbered in the LCC fleet, the latter having operated Leyton's tramways since 1921.
Modern Transport/IAL

Above: At the end of the vestibule-front trial the two-louvre, no-wiper style of windscreen was judged to be the best, and in August 1931 it was decided to fit similar screens to all suitable cars. 'E/3' No 2001 was chosen to model the new front for the press, but quite what it was full of we shall never know.
London Transport Museum

Left: After one year in service the 'E/3s' still looked very smart. No 1922 is seen on the Embankment in July 1931, before having its vestibule front fitted.
G. N. Southernden/HCV Collection — L .B. Newham Library Service

Right: Less than two months in service, LCC No 1 was photographed at The Angel, Islington, working subway route 33. The car looks in keeping with the bus alongside, but a world apart from the two trams behind.
G. N. Southernden/HCV Collection — L .B. Newham Library Service

appreciated by the travelling public. ... The interior decorations have been carried out in a particularly neat and simple manner on modern lines. There is an entire absence of mouldings or awkward corners where dirt might accumulate; in fact, the first impression we gained was the completely clean and wholesome appearance of car interiors from ceilings to floors.'

By 5 March 1931, 136 of the 150 new cars were reported to be in service, with the rest following shortly afterwards.

In December 1929, towards the end of Joshua Bruce's time as General Manager, the LCC announced that it had allocated £5,000 for the development and construction of an experimental bogie tramcar of an improved design. As with the concurrent developments on the MET, the design took advantage of recent experience. The first ideas were sketched out in January 1930, but the project was spurred along when Theodore Thomas became General Manager, many ideas being said to have come

from his fertile mind. Experience with 112 'HR/2' cars now in service had shown the advantages of four-motor/equal-wheel bogies and all-metal bodies. Experiments with vestibule fronts had also shown the strength and versatility of 'Alpax' aluminium, which the new car used for the window frames on the upper deck. Someone also had a good working knowledge of the MET and LUT 'Felthams', as the new car featured an on-one-level lower deck, and air-operated brakes and doors.

Given the number 1 in the LCC fleet, the new car entered service on the Kingsway Subway routes 31, 33 and 35 in the week beginning 9 May 1932:
'Outwardly the car is distinguished by its blue and white finish and stream-line effect. Parts that project on the standard car — such as vestibules, indicator boxes, side destination boards and headlamps — are built into the body. Folding doors on both platforms give finish to those features and, in addition, make it possible to accommodate standing passengers in

Left: A view of the driver's cab — 'A' end — of LCC No 1. The driver's pedestal seat was removed for the photograph to be taken. The stairs lead off immediately behind the driver's cab to the left, whilst to the right the depth of the upholstery on the seats is in marked contrast to that on other LCC cars.
Modern Transport/IAL

Below left: The upper deck of LCC No 1. Experience with 'Alpax' aluminium on vestibule fronts had shown the strength and versatility of the material, which was used to form the window frames on the upper deck of the experimental car. The recessed lighting used on the car is also seen clearly in this view.
Modern Transport/IAL

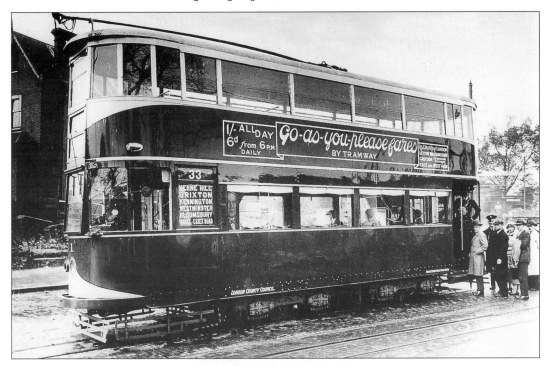

Above: LCC No 1 'Bluebird' in service on Kingsway Subway route 33 in November 1932. Its livery makes the car look more streamlined than it really is. The cameraman has, unfortunately, interrupted the efficient rear loading of the car.
National Tramway Museum

Right: In early LPTB days, with a cart to its right and an old van to its left, LCC No 1 looks oddly out of place as it works the 35A route — Highbury–Elephant & Castle — introduced on 1 June 1933. *Rev Helen Mace/ National Tramway Museum*

LCC No 1 remained in regular service until just after the war started, when it was put into store. After enjoying favour for charter by enthusiasts, in 1951 the car was sold to Leeds, in lieu of two 'Felthams' lost in a fire before they could be transported there. No 1 became No 301 in Leeds, and remained in service until September 1957. It is seen at Chapeltown on 3 October 1954. *D. Trevor Rowe/IAL*

comfort at one end of the car, just behind the driver. ... The interior of the car has been planned to provide maximum seating comfort, electric lighting of the diffuse type and tubular electric heaters operated from the line supply and so arranged that sections may be varied to produce the desired temperature. Seats number 28 in the lower saloon and 38 in the upper. All seats are not only of the armchair type but are in pairs, with reversible backs. The upholstery is of blue moquette, with panels of Rexine. ... While the car is in service the rear door is open and the front door closed. ... The car has an acceleration of 3.5ft per second and a maximum speed of 30 mph.'

Owing to its predominantly-blue livery, No 1 was nicknamed 'Bluebird'. The car remained in regular service until just after the outbreak of war in 1939, when it was withdrawn and put into store. When final closure of the tramways became imminent, and especially after Operation Tramaway was announced, No 1 became popular for charter by enthusiasts, and in this way it saw use on more of the remaining tramway system than it ever had before. In 1951 the car was sold to Leeds, in lieu of two 'Felthams' lost in a fire before they could be transported there. In Leeds No 1 became No 301, and remained in service until September 1957. It is now preserved at the National Tramway Museum.

10. The 'Big Five' — The formation of the LPTB

During the Great War, the Government took a measure of control over the country's railways, in order to ensure the ready movement of troops, munitions and supplies. When the war ended, some in Government were reluctant to relinquish this control, which manifested itself in the creation of an all-embracing 'Ministry of Transport' in 1919. In the discussions and negotiations that followed, nationalisation was much in the air, advocated most strongly by the MP Herbert Morrison, who wanted to see all public transport in London included in any such proposals. Ultimately a compromise was reached under which 123 railway companies were 'grouped' into the 'Big Four', and London's transport was allowed to continue as before — for the moment. A Select Committee was set up to look into congestion in the existing means of transport in the metropolitan area, and throughout the 1920s a search was on for ways of co-ordinating London's public transport.

The election of a Labour Government on 30 May 1929 led to Herbert Morrison being given the post of Minister of Transport. Now he had both the scope and authority to return to his goal of unifying London's transport. Morrison outlined his proposals on 2 December 1929. He sought:

- unification under public control
- management by a non-political body
- participation by the main line railway companies, and
- a self-supporting, unsubsidised system to be run commercially.

On 2 October 1930 Herbert Morrison made a more detailed statement of his proposals, ahead of the publication on 13 March 1931 of a Bill to be put before Parliament:

'... details of the Government Bill for the co-ordination of London's traffic have become known. This entails the appointment of a body to be known as the LONDON PASSENGER TRANSPORT BOARD composed of five "persons who have had wide experience and have shown capacity on transport, industry, commerce or finance, and in the conduct of public affairs". They may be appointed for a period of up to seven years. About £130,000,000 of capital is involved in the existing undertakings which it is proposed to transfer to the Board. The "Big Five" will co-ordinate London traffic within a twenty-five mile radius of Charing Cross. They will take over the Tube Railways, Metropolitan District Railway, and Metropolitan Railway, all tramway undertakings in the London area, the London General Omnibus Company, and the London omnibus businesses of other proprietors. The Board will not take over the suburban lines of the four amalgamated railway companies, but special arrangements are proposed for promoting co-ordination of the suburban services of these Companies with those taken over by the Board, by the avoidance of wasteful competition and affording opportunity for pooling receipts from competitive traffic. ... The "Big Five" will be given power to borrow and issue stock. The Minister of Transport has decided that there shall be no subsidy from public funds. London traffic must pay for itself.'

Two years of debate and bargaining followed, notably with the Underground Group, but the Bill was eventually presented to Parliament and gained Royal Assent on 13 April 1933. Vesting day for the new authority was set for 1 July 1933, and the handing-over of the various undertakings was met with due ceremony. At a meeting of Ilford Town Council on 27 June a letter of resignation from Mr L. E. Harvey, the Tramways Manager, was read out in which he expressed 'regret at my severance with the

Council, with which I have been associated for over 20 years. I view with satisfaction and pride the part I and my staff have taken for many years in contributing towards the successful operation of the department, which is now to terminate in substantial advantage to the ratepayers of Ilford in the future.' The Council recorded its appreciation of the loyal and efficient services rendered by Mr Harvey and his staff.

At Thornton Heath depot, Croydon, on 29 June, a farewell meeting was held in the large workshop, attended by a considerable number of past and present employees, including several men whose records went back to horse tram days. The Mayor, Councillor Carpenter, said that he 'expects that many of the men will view the change with some concern and some doubts and suspicions as to their own futures. You must remember however that some of the greatest troubles in life were the things which never happened. It might be that the change will work out for the welfare of all concerned. I believe that your lives will go on just the same as before and that you will hardly recognise that a change has taken place. I can assure you that the people of Croydon appreciate the loyal services of the tramway men and join with me in wishing them good luck and happiness in the future.'

The LCC marked the occasion with a dinner at County Hall, hosted by the Chairman of the Highways Committee, Councillor F. Bertram Galer. Replying to the toast of 'the LCC', Lord Ashfield, the Chairman of the new LPTB, said that 'it is unfortunate that the Board starts upon its career at a time when conditions are falling and the increased earnings are not sufficient to meet the burden of capital expenditure. The position facing the Board is one which I could have wished had been happier, but encouraged by the support of the public and the Council the Board approaches its task believing that the scheme can not and would not fail.'

Far left: This is how the newly-empowered LPTB declared itself to the world in the trade press. The stylish logo did not catch on. *IAL*

Left: Within a year the logo had been replaced by the more familiar roundel device, adapted from that used by the former Underground Group. *IAL*

At the changeover, which took place over a weekend, the task of obliterating the existing identity marks on the buses, trams and trolleybuses was completed, and by the start of the Board's first week of operation all vehicles had the name of their new owner painted on their sides.

Management of the tramways under the new London Passenger Transport Board (LPTB) was divided between the Northern and Western areas, which were under the charge of Christopher Spencer, late of the LUT, and the Central, Southern and Eastern areas, which were under the charge of Theodore Thomas, latterly General Manager of the LCC Tramways. Spencer resigned in mid-October 1933, leaving Thomas in overall control. At this time he made his views on the future of the tramways known: 'I do not think it would be right to anticipate the early disappearance of the trams, as a whole, as many are new or in good condition, but I think the Board is alive to the situation and to the need for making changes in a number of places. ... It must be obvious to anyone that the outlying parts of London's tramway system must be changed to something more suitable. In some districts the tramways are in very poor condition. On the other hand some routes — such as the Embankment — are satisfactorily served by trams. It is a big problem to tackle.'

In 1934 the LPTB announced a policy to replace trams with trolleybuses in the outer areas. The Board favoured trolleybuses as they seated 70, nearer to the capacity of a tram and more than the then-available motorbuses, which seated only 56. A Bill to permit the conversion of tramways to trolleybus operation gained the Royal Assent on 31 July 1934, and the first conversion, of three former LUT tramway routes in North London, took place on 27 October 1935. The conversion of the tramways serving Enfield on 8 May 1938 marked a turning-point in this programme, for it gave London more miles of trolleybus routes than it had miles of tramway routes left.

Despite the war the conversion programme was completed, with the final stage taking effect on 9 July 1940. The changes left North London with very few tramway routes. A similar programme to convert South London's

Left: Of the former Borough tramcars included in the LPTB fleet, some of the most striking were ex-Croydon bogie cars Nos 21-30, which became LPTB Nos 365-374. Not conduit-fitted, the cars remained on their old haunt, the Thornton Heath route, which lay entirely within the Borough. Here car No 370 (ex-No 26) is seen working the Thornton Heath route, 42. The cars were withdrawn and scrapped in December 1936. *V. C. Jones/IAL*

Centre left: The LPTB inherited 52 cars from the former SMET system. Seen as having a short working life, they were not renumbered into the main fleet, but given the suffix 's' after their original fleetnumbers. Here No 40s, still in SMET livery but with its new ownership on each side, waits to work to the Crystal Palace. The cars were withdrawn on 9 February 1936, when they were replaced by trolleybuses, depriving Londoners of the opportunity to ride on an open-top double-deck tram. Before the year was out, the Crystal Palace too was no more, having burned down on the night of 30 November.
H. F. Wheeler/R. S. Carpenter

Below left: Some of the first experiments in rehabilitating former LCC 'E/1' tramcars saw the restyling of the upper decks to resemble the 'Feltham' cars and the experimental LCC car, No 1. No 1103 emerged in this new form in January 1935. Passengers probably noticed the new seats most of all. In the lower saloon they were single rotating ones, and in the upper saloon double revolving ones. The car is seen in the early 1950s. *V. C. Jones/IAL*

tramways to trolleybuses, scheduled to commence on 1 October 1940, was, however, postponed until after the war. The North London closures robbed the Capital of much of its tramway diversity; most of the cars withdrawn as part of the closures were those from the former private undertakings: the LUT, MET and SMET. As a result, London saw its last open-top double-deck trams when the former SMET West Croydon-Crystal Palace route closed on 8 February 1936, and its last single-deckers when the former MET Alexandra Palace route — which included the line of the Alexandra Palace Railway, London's first overhead electric tramway — closed on 23 February 1938.

Theodore Thomas was also true to his word with regard to some of the tramcar fleet, especially the ex-LCC cars. Many of them were 'new or in good condition', and, between April 1934 and July 1935, 13 'E' or 'E/1' class cars were 'rehabilitated' at Charlton Works. This work amounted to almost a rebuilding, certainly for the bodies, which received new panels and styling, windscreens, plus refitted interiors and new seating. Deemed a success, between November 1935 and October 1936 a further 152 cars were rehabilitated in a similar manner, again mainly 'E/1s', but also including six 'HR/2s' and four ex-Croydon cars.

The LPTB also sold a few trams on to other authorities, Sunderland purchasing former MET experimental 'Feltham' No 331 in 1936, and Leeds acquiring three 'HR/2' cars in 1939.

Above: One of the experimental rehabilitations of former LCC tramcars involved the near-rebuilding of car No 1370, which had been severely damaged in an accident on 3 June 1933. The new car had been radically restyled to resemble ex-LCC No 1 'Bluebird', especially on the upper deck, and was renumbered 2. Flush side panels and a recessed route-indicator box are prominent in this view of one platform. Note the spare plough beneath the stairs. *Modern Transport/IAL*

Right: More typical of the rehabilitated 'E/1' cars was No 1038, another of the experimental ones, which was outshopped from Charlton Works in this pristine condition in January 1935. With slight modifications, the more major rehabilitation programme which followed later in the year produced cars to this pattern. *Modern Transport/IAL*

Left: Most of the other former LCC trams at least received windscreens, but a few cars failed to have even these fitted. One was No 1497, seen in Well Hall Road, Eltham, on 22 October 1936. Note the line ears remaining in the span wires for holding the double overhead wires formerly in use on this route.
H. F. Wheeler/R. S. Carpenter

Centre left: Closure of the former SMET West Croydon–Crystal Palace route on 8 February 1936 denied Londoners the pleasure of an open-topped tram ride. The backs of the seats on the upper decks of these cars had pull-down sheets on rollers that could be used to cover the knees in the rain! On 21 August 1935 LPTB No 346 (ex-Croydon No 2) waits at Crystal Palace terminus for the crowds who have been to the Exhibition of Mural Paintings there. Opposite, a group of men have asked some young ladies for the time, whilst a long bamboo pole, for turning the trolley heads round, hangs from the traction column. *A. D. Packer/ National Tramway Museum*

Below left: Low bridges on the former MET route to Alexandra Palace required the use of 15 single-deck cars, which the company classed as Type E. In LPTB days the service was maintained by an ever-dwindling number of these cars, until its closure on 23 February 1938, which also marked the last use of single-deckers on London Transport tramways in the 20th century. Here, in 1930, MET No 131 (later LPTB No 2302) waits at Alexandra Palace.
Dr Hugh Nicol/Science Museum

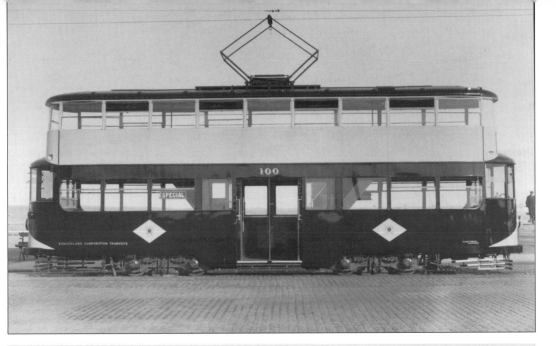

Above: The LPTB sold some of its tramcars on to other undertakings. No 2168 — ex-MET No 331 — was the last of the experimental designs for the 'Felthams'. With non-standard equipment, the car was withdrawn from service in August 1936 and sold to Sunderland Corporation in January 1937, where it became No 100 in that fleet. Spasmodic use in later years, followed by a period in store, meant that the car outlasted the closure of the Sunderland Tramways in 1954 and allowed it to be preserved. *IAL*

Below: Towards the end of 1939 the LPTB sold three 'HR/2' class cars — Nos 1881, 1883 and 1886 — to Leeds. This is how they were transported. The journey began at Woolwich, and took 2½ days, being increased by 73 miles to avoid low bridges. When incorporated into the Leeds Corporation fleet, this car became No 278. *Modern Transport/IAL*

Left: Leeds Corporation made a number of modifications to the ex-London 'HR/2' cars it bought in 1939, as shown on No 279 (ex-LPTB No 1886). Fitting a standard Leeds bow collector is one obvious change, as is the use of a livery that enhances the car's lines. Less obvious in this view was the replacement of a solid panel by the stairs next to the windscreen with a window, which allowed more light into the vestibules. *V. C. Jones/IAL*

Below: After the war, following the completion of Stage 3 of Operation Tramaway on 7 April 1951, the bulk of the former LUT and MET 'Felthams' were also sold to Leeds, where most worked until closure of that system on 7 November 1959. As Nos 515 (ex-LPTB No 2093) and 505 (ex-LPTB No 2069) in the Leeds fleet, two of the cars are seen in different liveries. Over 20 years after their introduction, they still looked modern. *IAL*

11. Elephant's memory —
The making of
The Elephant Will Never Forget

By the late 1930s the LPTB had practically completed the conversion to trolleybus operation of all its tram routes in West, North and East London. To follow on from this, it had planned a similar programme of tramway abandonment and conversion to trolleybuses for the remaining tram routes in South London. The name 'Operation Tramaway' was coined for this programme, which was scheduled to start on 1 October 1940. Due to the war, this programme was shelved, but was revived to begin 10 years later to the day — this time in favour of motorbuses, rather than trolleybuses.

As word of the final abandonment of London's trams spread, enthusiasts made every effort to photograph, film and record what they could, and the last three to four years of London's tramways are probably the best documented of all. Perhaps the best-known record of London's trams is a short documentary film made by British Transport Films for the London Transport Executive in the final week of tramway operation. Taking its title from the famous inn sign at the once-busy tramway junction at the Elephant & Castle, the film was called *The Elephant Will Never Forget*.

British Transport Films (BTF) had been formed in January 1949 as the film-production arm of the British Transport Commission, the body which oversaw the newly-nationalised transport undertakings: British Waterways, London Transport, British Railways and British Road Services (BRS), plus those bus companies formerly owned by Tilling and Balfour-Beatty. In charge of production at BTF was Edgar Anstey, who had been trained by the founder of the British documentary film movement, John Grierson, at the Empire Marketing Board and GPO film units. Work for Shell, the March of Time in the USA, and the Ministry of Information during the war had given Anstey a wide range of experience, and he welcomed the BTF post as it gave him the broad remit that Grierson had enjoyed at the GPO in the early 1930s.

In 1950 BTF took over responsibility for the production of the *Cine Gazette* series of information newsreels from London Transport's own film unit, which was now disbanded. In an interview on 13 November 1986, Edgar Anstey

One of the first tram-replacement buses works along the tramlines on the Embankment in October 1950, whilst 11 passengers wait for the next tram. The availability of these buses allowed Operation Tramaway to resume on 1 October 1950, exactly 10 years after it was originally intended to. *Modern Transport/IAL*

recalled how *The Elephant Will Never Forget* came to be made:

'BTF were doing a lot of films for LT at the time, and I was informed in the usual way that the last tram was due to run. I had an idea that this might be a nostalgic thing to do and so I talked to John Krish about it. Our next inspiration was The Players' Theatre. There was a chap there who sang Cockney songs brilliantly. Perhaps the famous tram song from the Victorian Music Halls could be used in the film in some way. And so we thought about it — what I suppose would today be called brainstorming — and we came up with nostalgia for the war, the rain in south London, and the rhythm of that song. We became very excited by it — we thought it might win us an award. It was certainly the first film to receive attention. John Krish was the perfect person for that, he had a romantic approach which suited the material well.'

Given the working title 'Trams', BTF production No 108 was planned in the early months of 1952. The production notes survive in the London Transport Museum, from which the following schedule of dates and locations has been derived:

Reel	Date	Locations
1	4 April 1952	Kingsway 'Tunnel' and Embankment
2	8 April 1952	Kingsway
3	1 July 1952	New Cross Depot Siemens Works, Woolwich night scenes at Elephant & Castle
4	1 July 1952	night scenes at Westminster Bridge Old Kent Road
5	2 July 1952	Old Kent Road/Westminster Bridge — tram approaching camera New Cross Depot Deptford New Cross Westminster Bridge Night scenes at Blackfriars Bridge
6	3 July 1952	Woolwich — workers boarding trams in the rain outside Siemens Works, Woolwich trams in rain in Woolwich re-takes of night scenes at Blackfriars Bridge from Reel 5, plus night scenes on Embankment
7	4 July 1952	tram lines at Woolwich Free Ferry, Savoy Street, Brockley via Old Kent Road, City and Southwark via Old Kent Road/Westminster — all from behind driver close-ups of trams Darby & Joan couple sequence in Old Kent Road, over Blackfriars Bridge and with conductor
8	4 July 1952	Darby & Joan couple with conductor Inspectors timing trams in New Cross Street Darby & Joan couple talking — Festival Hall in background Darby & Joan couple with conductor pointsman outside New Cross Depot tram interior — conductor switches on lights, people take their seats, conductor takes fares various passengers getting on and off trams
9	5 July 1952	Tram lower deck — passengers, conductor, tramspotters frustrated driver (from inside a BTC-owned Humber) Beresford Square pawnbroker and market shots plough-changing at Woolwich Free Ferry (many shots) raising pole to overhead (many shots)

		Embankment St Paul's Cathedral
10	5 July 1952	closing ceremony
11	5 July 1952	closing ceremony 2nd camera — all shots spoiled, scratched and out of focus
12	7 July 1952	'Tram Stop' signs
13	11 July 1952	'Last Tram' poster, tram being pushed
14	1 Sept 1952	trams being scrapped at Charlton
15	21 Feb 1953	'Elephant & Castle' inn sign

Post-production work on the film was undertaken between August 1952 and May 1953, as the following schedule shows:

15 August 1952	sound dubbing
16 December 1952	music recording
31 January 1953	recording Archie Harradine singing 'Riding on Top of the Car'
25 March 1953	music dubbing
1 May 1953	music dubbing
13 May 1953	dubbing music over *Cine Gazette* titles
19 May 1953	dubbing horn solo

One of the most evocative elements in the film is the music, which was especially composed for it by Edward Williams. He used themes from the Music Hall song 'Riding on Top of the Car'. The song itself was featured in the film, in a rendition by Archie Harradine and the Lewisham Darby & Joan Club. Edgar Anstey recalled that Harradine 'had an awful stammer — he could hardly speak at all in fact — but once the music started he could sing perfectly'.

Rumours persist of opposition to the film from within London Transport. John Krish was criticised for over-shooting on what was a small film, but he could hardly have been expected to re-shoot the material in the event of a problem, such as that which bedevilled the second camera rostered to cover the closing ceremony. The tone of the film was also said to be overly sentimental, and here there is evidence of last-minute changes to the spoken narration. Reproduced here, for the first time, is the narration script for *The Elephant Will Never Forget*, as preserved in the London Transport Museum.

Words in the script that do not appear in the film are shown in italics within brackets. Words that appear in the film, but are not included in the script, are shown in bold. Frames and production stills from the film are not available, but similar images have been chosen to illustrate appropriate points in the script:

THE ELEPHANT WILL NEVER FORGET

[*There is something missing South of the Thames. Down there every street one way or another seems to lead to the Elephant and Castle. The pub sign still stands above the traffic, but the Elephant has lost a friend.*]

(Narration replaced by caption:)
At the hub of South London the famous inn sign still stands high above the traffic, but in the streets below something is missing....

MAIN TITLE: THE ELEPHANT WILL NEVER FORGET

[*The Elephant and the trams belonged together. But*] **It was one day, not long ago, London had to say goodbye to her last tram**. sometime someday it had to come — and some people were glad to see the back of them, and some of us were sorry they were going — for we'd be missing a sight as friendly as a Pleasure Steamer — though not quite so silent...

EFFECTS SEQUENCE

One last week to clatter through the streets — streets that will never be the same now the tram is gone, now all the paraphernalia that was only theirs is in the attic.

Those stops for the change from the middle rail to the overheads — where the conductor

'It was one day, not long ago, London had to say goodbye to her last tram ... .' 'E/3' class car No 2000 crosses Westminster Bridge on 5 July 1952, adorned with chalked inscriptions: 'R.I.P.', 'The Last Round-up', 'Our Last Call'. *D. Sutton Collection/IAL*

aimed the arm and got it up first time, most times.

A hundred yards away the ploughmen, on their own little island. Out would shoot the plough for the trams going the other way. Under it would go the fork to help it slide in. Down would come the arm, and the change was complete. And that's how it was every day, give and take like an old married couple.

The drivers, conductors, the depotmen and linesmen and the ploughman and the pointsmen share with some of us an affection for the old ladies, [*who, it must be admitted, had sometimes gone off the rails, were always going round the bend and yet keeping when they could to the straight and narrow.*]

We'll remember the rattle and the clang and the sway, and how snug it was to be inside when it was raining outside.

It's a funny thing really but the trams and the rain and the streets of South London all seem to belong together — not that anyone likes getting wet — not that now the trams have gone the weather'll be brighter — it's just that they belong together, [*like the pier and the mud at Southend ...*]

And to see them going by those corners that haven't been built on since the bombing. **Ah** They seem a long way off now, those days of the Blitz.

That sound of the first morning tram used to

'Under it would go the fork to help it slide in ... .' Ex-East Ham car No 98 works towards the City on route 46 during the last week of tramway operation. *F. M. Usset/IAL*

'That sound of the first morning tram used to be a comfort all right then … .' 'E/1' class car No 1316 works along Beresford Street, Woolwich, towards the Free Ferry, en route to Abbey Wood, passing a theatre, the 'Ready Snax' cafe, and the 'Gay Adventure' bar. *V. C. Jones/IAL*

be a comfort all right then — you'd hear it long before the All Clear sometimes — [*and it was the sound of Life picking itself up after the night before — when you came off duty or out of the shelter wiping the lack of sleep from your eyes to see whether the view was the same…*]

And the people who welcomed the tram then and miss them most now they are gone are the Cockneys.

They'll remember the shilling all day, and what a lovely ride it was — right round London and underneath, before, that is, the Kingsway Tunnel was closed.

Oh The trams were theirs all right, and fifty years ago they even used to sing about them in the Music Halls …

RIDING ON TOP OF THE CAR

[*The last week is almost over.*] This is their last but one night — twenty four hours from now the tram[s] would be dead. And when the daylight of that last day came the old trams were blinking in the sun and standing like mourners at their own funerals.

They weren't to know that Londoners were that night going to give them a sendoff the American President might envy.

In the day though, the children were having

'They'll remember the shilling all day, and what a lovely ride it was — right round London and underneath, before, that is, the Kingsway Tunnel was closed … .' 'E/3' class car No 1928 emerges blinking into the daylight from the southern end of the Kingsway Subway, beneath a portal of Waterloo Bridge. *V. C. Jones/IAL*

Above: 'The Tramspotters turned out to the last man. Backwards and forwards round and round they were riding just to get as many numbers as they possibly could ... .' Last Tram Day graffiti ranged from the banal to the prosaic. This is one of the better efforts: 'Much to our delight and your sorrow we really can't come round tomorrow'. *D. Sutton Collection/IAL*

Below: 'The motorist who every day cursed every time he had to stop, cursed but little and looked forward to tomorrow. ...' Ex-Walthamstow 'E/1' No 2058 and 'E/1' car No 1782 pass near the Borough terminus on 27 June 1951. Although it operated until final closure, route 72 was cut back to the Embankment with the end of Stage 4 of Operation Tramaway on 10 July 1951. *V. C. Jones/IAL*

their moneysworth. The Tramspotters turned out to the last man. Backwards and forwards round and round they were riding just to get as many numbers as they possibly could, [*for as morning turned to afternoon the trams were retiring one by one into the break up yard.*]

The motorist who every day cursed every time he had to stop, cursed but little and looked forward to tomorrow.

Past the Pawnbrokers and through the Street Markets [— *from the days when London had four hundred trams to this day, it is where they belonged,*] but now only for a few more hours [— *for as afternoon turned to evening the last twenty were making their last journey.*]

And what was the Tram Driver thinking — that man who stood with his back to us and whose face we probably never saw.

Remembering and thinking. Thinking of the day after tomorrow when the trams will be picked clean of all their value, and the shells sold to the scrappers who'll start the breaking up, [*and if the wind is in the right direction — burn them.*]

Perhaps he's remembering the days before yesterday — when the first tram ever appeared. The stories his father used to tell, or how he himself started as a conductor in 1910, punching tickets at night by the flickering light of an oil lamp, [*and how when you've been on trams so long you come to know every cobble in the road.*

'Past the Pawnbrokers and through the Street Markets, but now only for a few more hours ... .' An ex-West Ham car, No 337, picks its way through Beresford Square, Woolwich, in the evening sunlight. Ahead is the imposing entrance to Woolwich Arsenal, now an isolated and forlorn ruin. *V. C. Jones/IAL*

'And what was the Tram Driver thinking — that man who stood with his back to us ... ?' *V. C. Jones/IAL*

'... Remembering and thinking. Thinking of the day after tomorrow when the trams will be picked clean of all their value, and the shells sold to the scrappers who'll start the breaking up.' Withdrawn for scrap after Stage 1 of Operation Tramaway in October 1950, 'E/1' class car No 1385 awaits its fate at Penhall Road. This car had been rehabilitated in March 1936. *IAL*

No more early summer mornings on the Embankment and taking aboard the Coster Women and their baskets of flowers fresh from Covent Garden.]

It all started a long time ago and now it's the finish.

The way they burn them till there's nothing left but a charred skeleton — you'd think they were afraid of Ghosts — Ghosts of Old Trams running the rails at night.

Oh well, in thirty six hours he'll be a bus driver, and for the first time in forty two years he'**ll** [d] be sitting down ...

NIGHT SCENES

Oh what a night that was — London hung on to its Last Tram like a dog with an old bone — and at New Cross Depot Lord Latham, the Chairman of London Transport, could only wait and wait, until at last London, let go, said Goodbye, and allowed it into the Depot for the triumphant and ceremonial very last run in.

And the man who drove it in? — John Cliff the deputy Chairman, who fifty-two years ago started as a Tramwayman ...

'Oh what a night that was — London hung on to its Last Tram like a dog with an old bone ... .' Southwark Bridge, 11pm, 5 July 1952: ghostly figures surround a policeman as he attends the departure of ex-West Ham car No 337 — the last car to work from this terminus. The beading on the upper deck prevented these cars from carrying the familiar 'LAST TRAM WEEK' banners. *C. Carter/IAL*

THE CEREMONY

AULD LANG SYNE

The Party was over — and Londoners, twenty thousand of them somehow made their way home — it was too early in the morning for the buses — and the next tram had gone.

[*So London quietened down.*]

THE END

FAREWELL   TO   LONDON'S   TRAMS

The Chairman and Members of the

LONDON TRANSPORT EXECUTIVE

request the pleasure of the company of

....

at 11 p.m. on Saturday, 5th July, 1952, at

NEW CROSS TRAM DEPOT

on the completion of the work of converting

the Tramway System to Bus Operation.

R.S.V.P.
The Chief Public Relations Officer
London Transport, 55 Broadway, S.W.1   P.T.O.

'... and at New Cross Depot Lord Latham, the Chairman of London Transport, could only wait and wait ... .' Some of the people who waited with Lord Latham for the last tram to arrive were there by invitation. Surely no one turned up uninvited? *Author's collection*

The end credits also note that the photography was by Bob Paynter and the editing by Jack Ellitt, but the narrator's name is not given. Edgar Anstey kindly tracked this information down in 1986, and so, in the style of the film commentary: 'And the man who narrated it — Brewster Mason'.

12. Trams beat jams — Croydon Tramlink, the next generation of London trams

Croydon's last tram ran in the early hours of 8 April 1951, the closure forming part of Stage 3 of Operation Tramaway. With the final route closures in July 1952, any ideas of trams being reintroduced into Croydon, or to any other part of Greater London, seemed fanciful in the extreme. But the world turns, and it was a study of transport in Greater London, carried out by London Transport and British Rail and published in 1986, that first suggested a tram scheme to serve the town. From 1990 Croydon Council and London Transport worked to promote a light rail scheme called Tramlink.

Public consultations took place during 1991, discussing routes and testing public feeling — 80% of those asked felt Tramlink was a good idea. Three routes were chosen:

1 — Wimbledon–Croydon–Elmers End
2 — Croydon–Beckenham Junction
3 — Croydon–New Addington.

All three utilised parts of former railway lines, and were linked through the centre of Croydon on a street-running loop that connected East and West Croydon stations, forming a 17½-mile system. A Bill was drawn up, and in November 1991 it was put to Parliament. Some amendments were made and the Croydon Tramlink Act received Royal Assent on 21 July 1994, giving London Regional Transport (LRT) legal powers to build and run Tramlink.

Whilst Parliament was considering the Bill, Croydon Council, LRT and three private companies worked together to start the design process. This group was disbanded in 1995 when Tramlink went out to tender across Europe. As with many new schemes, the contract available was a design/build/finance/operate concession. The successful consortium

Memories of Croydon's first generation of trams: 1. Ex-Croydon Corporation car No 44 (LPTB No 388) works the 42 route to Thornton Heath. Wholly within Croydon, the route retained ex-Corporation cars to the end. On 17 December 1949, No 388 is caught in the low winter sun. *V. C. Jones/IAL*

Memories of Croydon's first generation of trams: 2. At Thornton Heath terminus, ex-Corporation car No 40 (LPTB No 384) seems to be in two minds as to where to go next, although its options seem limited in at least one direction. *V. C. Jones/IAL*

was Tramtrack Croydon Ltd (TCL), which included:

- CentreWest London Buses Ltd (part of FirstGroup) — responsible for operation and maintenance of the system;
- Bombardier EuroRail — responsible for designing and building the trams;
- Royal Bank of Scotland and 3i — responsible for the finance; and
- Sir Robert McAlpine/Amey Construction Ltd — responsible for constructing the system.

The total capital cost was around £200 million, of which £125 million was provided by Central Government in recognition of the benefit to other road users and the easing of congestion. Construction work started in January 1997.

Of all the UK's new light rail/tramway schemes (Manchester Metrolink, Sheffield Supertram, Midland Metro), Croydon Tramlink is the first to have its whole progress charted on the Internet. The consortium had its own website

(www.tramlink.uk.com), which contained online versions of its publicity material. Although informative, this site was not updated very often. Most people trying to keep up to date with developments in Croydon turned to an unofficial website started by local resident Steven Parascandolo (www.croydontramlink.co.uk). He was interested in setting up a website, and the growing tramway in his local streets seemed an ideal subject for one.

The following descriptions are taken, with permission, from this website. They have an immediacy that is in keeping with the other contemporary accounts in this book.

On entering the website there is an introductory message:

'This unofficial site was set up in February 1999 and has followed the development and now covers the operation of this fascinating system. The construction was complex and testing took a little longer than expected but the trams on all routes are now running and full of happy, fare paying passengers. The critics have fallen silent as the general population rather than just dedicated enthusiasts realised how good trams are for London.

'You can rarely travel far on the trams before you overhear more praise of them from ordinary passengers. They are fast, efficient and accessible and the staff are superb. This is a new kind of public transport showing what can be done if a little money and effort is put into a forward thinking vision of public transport. Tramlink hopes to get 2 million car journeys a year off of [sic] London's congested roads as well as 20 million passengers each year!

'Other Systems are being developed for other parts of London and the UK and these should be supported. Write to your MP, to ministers, to the Mayor of London and to newspapers. If you doubt the effectiveness of Light Rail, come to Croydon and see for yourselves what can be achieved.

'On this site, you should be able to find almost everything you want to know about Tramlink. It is aimed at both users of the system and tram enthusiasts as well as informing people about the history of the routes and fascinating Latest News reports of incidents, news, and gossip.'

Live testing of Croydon Tramlink in the town centre, by Her Majesty's Railway Inspectorate (HMRI), began on Wednesday 16 June 1999 — this is how it was reported on the website:

'Large crowds of photographers, camera crews, observers, Tramlink managers, the HMRI and others gathered at the "non-existent" time of 05:00 at the bottom of the Wandle Park Flyover. At 05:30, Tram 2535 descended the flyover into the centre under its own power for the first time. After a long pause under Jubilee Bridge for interviews with press, the Metropolitan Police Escort (4 bikes and 2 cars) got into position and with the Tramlink Operations Manager driving, the tram set off slowly around the loop. On board almost the whole front car was full of people. Police, HMRI, managers and representatives of Bombardier were all there. The first run around the loop stopped at almost every point of interest and caused some delay to following buses. Problems were encountered with tarmac and other materials on the rail heads causing some adhesion problems but generally the test went well. On reaching Dingwall Rd, the tram reversed through the George St Crossover and down through the town. A brake test was carried out on Crown Hill — The tram skidded somewhat! Plenty of staff were on hand to prevent cars from stopping in the path of the tram and the tram was preceded by the tow-away truck! After turning right at Reeves Corner, the tram did a second loop — much faster this time — before returning to sit under Jubilee bridge whilst staff got some breakfast (08:30). At about 09:00, the tram returned to the depot and news filtered through that the HMRI

Live testing of Croydon Tramlink in the town centre began on Wednesday 16 June 1999. Here car No 2535 swings round into Wellesley Road. As the unofficial Tramlink website reported, 'The first run around the loop stopped at almost every point of interest and caused some delay to following buses. Problems were encountered with tarmac and other materials on the rail heads causing some adhesion problems but generally the test went well.' *S. J. Parascandolo —* *www.croydontramlink.co.uk*

had refused further testing today and no more would take place tomorrow. I assume this is to enable the Rails to be cleaned thoroughly. One of the Staff on board was heard to say "Why didn't we think of cleaning off the tops of the rails?!" '

Opening was projected for November 1999, but various problems, such as current leakage, delayed this until May 2000. Once again, the unofficial website kept everyone informed of developments. This is how the opening of the first route, on 10 May 2000, was covered:

'The VIP Specials
    'VIPs travelled to New Addington by bus. After the ceremony, trams 2543 and 2530 worked two specials to Croydon. Both had flowers on the front. These ran one behind the other and left New Addington about 12:30. Meanwhile 2549 was waiting at Addiscombe and this took on invited enthusiasts (and a few others!) for a third VIP run to New Addington via Croydon. This did not take on passengers in Croydon. On arrival at New Addington, 2543 worked the first public departure from New Addington with 2550 ([in] FirstGroup [colours]) working the first public run from East Croydon. This was very busy.

'First Public Runs
    '2550 (FirstGroup) worked the first

Public tram from East Croydon at about 1300. The First Run from New Addington was with 2543. The public were allowed onto the VIP tram 3 (2549) back from New Addington complete with a good luck sign in the cab! The service was increased and trams were very busy throughout the afternoon. Wimbledon line trams (on driver training) were running through the Central section with "Not in Service" showing.

'The 04:29 — First Fare Paying Tram
    'Some of us got up early to do the first fare paying run at 04:29 on Thursday 11 May from West Croydon. 2540 arrived on time and we were surprised to find as many Revenue Inspectors as Passengers eager to check our tickets! The Tram arrived at New Addington at 04:52 to form the 04:55 to West Croydon. This was rather tiring especially for me as I updated the site at 23:00 on Wednesday, had 4 hours sleep and am still updating now (23:30 Thursday)!'

The second line to open was that to Beckenham on 23 May 2000:

'Beckenham was opened at a short Ceremony at Beckenham Junction at 10:45 on Tuesday 23 May 2000. The leader of Bromley Council cut the ribbon after making a short speech in which he wished the line success and also said that a

The opening ceremony for the first route of the Croydon Tramlink system on 10 May 2000. The Mayor of Croydon, Dr Shafi Khan, and former London Transport tram driver Fred Roberts cut the ribbon. *John Bradshaw*

feasibility study was underway into extending to Crystal Palace. After the ribbon was cut, tram 2548 took invited guests to Croydon and back. The same tram then formed the first public service, the 12:02 from Beckenham Junction. This was another party atmosphere with half the tram full of enthusiasts, many related to this site in some way. Unfortunately, it was not possible to offer free rides in the same way as the Addington Route.'

Croydon Tramlink's final route — oddly, route 1 — was opened on 30 May 2000:

'The Wimbledon to Elmers End route was opened in secret on 30 May 2000 by a small group of VIPs at Therapia Lane Staff Halt of all places. It is thought the opening was to have taken place at Merton Park but someone changed it! A ribbon was cut and the VIPs travelled on 2548 to Wimbledon stopping at Phipps Bridge for photos. After the VIPs had returned to Croydon, all trams

on the route started carrying passengers at 12:00. The First departure from Wimbledon was packed with enthusiasts and passengers and left at 12:00 with 2538. This line which uses parts of the former Railtrack Elmers End–Addiscombe and West Croydon– Wimbledon lines opened just a day short of 3 years since the last passenger trains and the final Connex Last In Last Out Railtour ran over these lines on 31 May 1997.'

Twenty-four trams operate Croydon Tramlink. In a move which gave a tangible link with London's first generation of trams, it was decided to number the fleet in sequence with the former LPTB one. On its formation the LPTB renumbered the trams acquired from the Underground Group, and some of the London Boroughs, to follow on from the highest-numbered car in the former LCC fleet — 'E/3' class car No 2003. The highest-numbered car in this new sequence was ex-LUT Type W car No 259, which became LPTB No 2529.

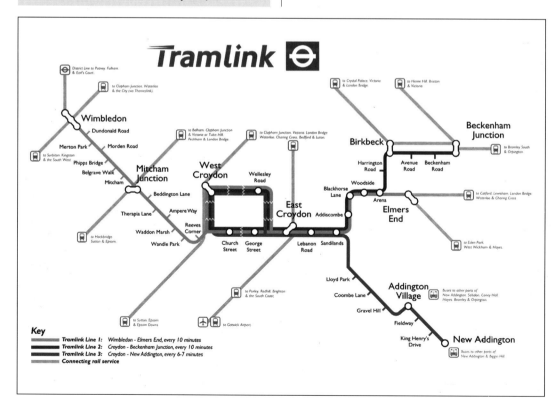

Thus the Croydon Tramlink trams are numbered from No 2530 onwards. In another link with the past, the generic livery for the Tramlink vehicles is red and white, close to the LPTB's red and cream.

The year 2000 saw the dawning of a new era in London's tramway history. Croydon Tramlink has proven itself, and already there is talk of new routes and extensions to the system, which should ensure that tramway historians of the future will have much to write about on the continuing history of London trams.

Left: A map of the Croydon Tramlink system.
Croydon Tramlink

Above: The Croydon Tramlink travels along streets which the town's former tramways also used. One such is Station Road, West Croydon. Here SMET car No 43 is seen loading in the early years of that system.
National Tramway Museum

Right: The buildings to the right are remarkably unaltered in this view of the same location on 23 July 2000. Tramlink car No 2542 is working the New Addington route. *Author*

Left: Cost-cutting is not always advisable. Just two months after opening, all four signs at Addiscombe station, common to the Beckenham and Elmers End routes, had unofficially renamed it 'disco'. The letters were individual vinyl ones that could be peeled off! *Author*

Centre left: At Sandilands station on 23 July 2000, Tramlink car No 2545 pulls in, working route 3 to New Addington. *Author*

Below left: Having reached its destination, Tramlink car No 2545 waits at New Addington to return to West Croydon. *Author*

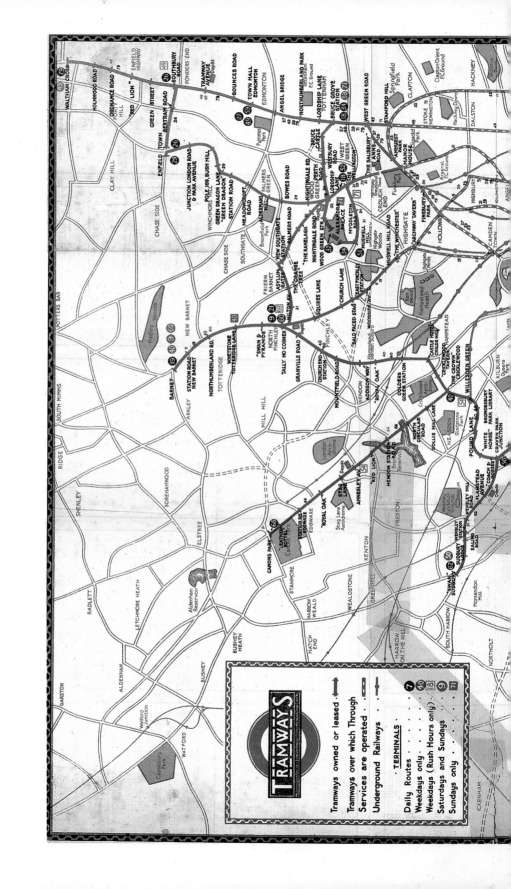